ARTISTIC TASTES

Favorite Recipes *of* Native American Artists

Collected by Barbara Harjo

Text by Julie Pearson Little Thunder

KIVA
PUBLISHING, INC.

FIRST EDITION
ISBN 1-885772-08-4

Publisher's Cataloging-in-Publication
(Provided by Quality Books, Inc.)

Harjo Barbara.
    Artistic tastes: favorite recipes of Native American
artists / collected by Barbara Harjo, text by Julie Pearson
Little Thunder. — I st ed.
        p. cm.
        Includes index.
        Preassigned LCCN: 98-85824
        ISBN: 1-885772-08-4

    1. Indian cookery. 2. Indians of North America—Food.
3. Indian artists—United States-Biography. 4. Cookery,
American—Southwestern style. 1. Little Thunder, Julie
Pearson. II. Title.
TX715.L58 1998   641.59'297
                    QB198-751

Cover art: *Peking Duck,* by Benjamin Harjo, Jr.
Cover design by David Skolkin Design Group
Text design by Rudy J. Ramos
Printed in USA by Ali Graphic Services, Inc.

9 8 7 6 5 4 3 2 1

8-98/7M/1998

DEDICATION

THIS BOOK IS DEDICATED to three very special women in my life—my grandmother, who is gone now, and two wild and beautiful heroines of mine, Jane and Ann. They all have played an important part in this process whether they know it or not.

I guess it all began in one of our kitchens, as most things do with us, Jane and I standing around talking, cooking, laughing, eating. Jane said something about doing a cookbook, and I thought, "What a brilliant idea!" We have all shared so much in the kitchen, with food being not just to sustain, but to fulfill, create and bond.

My grandmother's kitchen was like that—always a warm, safe haven. Grandmother was an amazing woman who worked all day and fed us melt-in-your-mouth wonders at night. She was the center of my life, and most of what I am today is thanks to her.

The idea for this cookbook stewed and simmered for some time before I got the encouragement I needed from my friend Ann, who knows everything. Feeling confident, I pitched it here and there for several years, until someone who could make it happen also liked the idea.

I would like to thank all my good friends who participated in the madness. I invite you to enjoy this piece of my life as much as I enjoyed watching it take on a life of its own. Savor each and every morsel with someone you love.

—Barbara Harjo

TABLE OF CONTENTS

Contents, continued

INTRODUCTION

SWEATLODGE OR POWWOW, peyote meeting or funeral, nothing happens in Indian country without the preparation and sharing of food. To this cultural foundation add the creativity and quirks of Indian artists—and you have the idea behind *Artistic Tastes.*

What connection does cooking have with art? As Merlin Little Thunder points out, "There's the palette and then there's the palate." Folks who wipe paintbrushes on their jeans or ceramic glaze on kitchen towels are not likely to be intimidated by the hands-on nature of cooking.

Not that everyone contributing to *Artistic Tastes* is an expert cook; some qualify for inclusion by being expert eaters. But even the non-cooks surprised us with insights into cooking and art, served up with dollops of humor and spirituality.

Being thankful for the plants and animals that provide our nourishment is a theme throughout this collection. But the Indian heritage of these artists can be traced in other ways, too, in various food taboos and favorite childhood meals—from wild onions to balogna sandwiches made with fresh piki bread.

Present-day food memories of these artists are likely to arise from cross-country trips to art shows and galleries. What makes an artist happy on Opening Night? Good sales, plenty of hors-d'oeuvres, and a sit-down dinner afterwards with artist friends. Because the bottom line in art is still the need to put food on the table. As Aleut sculptor Bill Prokopiof puts it, "If I don't create, I don't eat."

BEN DELLA

BEN DELLA'S LIFE—HIS REAL LIFE—BEGAN AT AGE TWENTY-TWO WHEN HE FIRST SET FOOT ON THE MAKAH RESERVATION. DELLA, WHO CAME FROM A MAKAH MEDICINE FAMILY, GREW UP IN CALIFORNIA. WHEN HE RETURNED TO HIS ANCESTRAL HOME, HE WAS WARMLY WELCOMED BY HIS PEOPLE, INCLUDING RELATIVES HE HAD NEVER MET.

"The medicine men were the carvers in our tribe," he explains. "When I got to the reservation, the first thing I did was talk to the elders. They showed me carving pieces my great-grandfather had made. Carving was in my blood. I picked it up right away."

Della, who never had art training in school, uses traditional Makah wood for his work. Red and yellow cedar, yew and alder have returned his devotion, yielding objects from rattles and masks to canoes. Acrylic paints or touches like abalone shell on a doll's eye add the finishing touches to his creations. "The wood talks to me," says Della. "As soon as I dive into that cedar, my spirit is in everything I do."

Thunderbird mask

Food as well as art, Della believes, can be used to teach Makah values. "Our food is fish. As a boy in Huntington Beach, I would stand on a stool when my father was cooking and ask all kinds of questions. I wanted to learn to cook the same things because they tasted so good!"

Central motifs in Della's work include food sources like salmon, whale and seal as well as totem animals. Totem poles are some of his most time-consuming creations, taking up to a year to complete. While some go to art collectors, others appear on reservations throughout the Pacific Northwest, spelling out clan and family ties.

While playing a lead role in the revival of Northwest Coast art, Della has kept his job with the Public Works Department of Salinas, California. Does the city itself have any of his carvings? "Not yet," he says, "But I'm talking to them about it."

"The spirit of my food helps me create."

Ben's Northwest Broiled Salmon

1 (6 pound) salmon

2 lemons

butter

salt and pepper to taste

Filet a six pound salmon, rinse well, cut in half and place in a baking pan. Slice two lemons and squirt over salmon. Allow to stand for one hour. Salt and pepper if you like.

Place under broiler for two minutes, then add a slice of butter for each piece of salmon and continue cooking for six minutes. Ready to serve.

Serves 4-6

Traditional Dried Smoked Salmon Soup

1 (6 pound) salmon

2 lemons

butter

salt and pepper to taste

Filet a six pound salmon, rinse well, cut in half and place in a baking pan. Slice two lemons and squirt over salmon. Allow to stand for one hour. Salt and pepper if you like.

Place under broiler for two minutes, then add a slice of butter for each piece of salmon and continue cooking for six minutes. Ready to serve.

Serves 4-6

MARCUS AMERMAN

THE DALAI LAMA, BROOKE SHIELDS, AND MARILYN MONROE ARE JUST A FEW OF THE SUBJECTS MARCUS AMERMAN HAS TACKLED IN BEAD-WORK. RAISED IN PHOENIX, ARIZONA, HE GRAVITATED TO THE INSTITUTE OF AMERICAN INDIAN ARTS IN SANTA FE, WHEN HIS COUSIN, LINDA LOMAHAFTEWA, STARTED TEACHING THERE.

Since then, he's developed a national reputation for his combination of painting and beadwork. But the Choctaw artist also explores other media. He recently designed a leather evening dress, with beadwork and a hundred parrot feathers. "It was very labor intensive in color and detail," says Amerman.

Always pushing the envelope, he created an installation/sculpture of glow-in-the-dark bulbs,

"I was extremely happy when I was upgraded from 'Starving Artist' to 'Struggling Artist.'"

laser lights and music at the IAIA Museum. The installation was noticed by native performance artist James Luna, who invited Amerman to perform with him during Indian Market. Their piece was called "Battle of the Network Shamans." Explains Amerman, "I was a technoshaman character, performing

Geronimo

my own rituals of spiritual rebirth and death, and filling in parts while Luna was dressing."

So far Amerman's schedule and his peripatetic lifestyle have kept him from exploring cooking in a serious way. But he is proud of his progression from starving to struggling artist. "A starving artist carries around cans in his suitcase," he observes wryly.

PESTO PIZZA

PESTO SAUCE:

2 cups fresh basil leaves

3 cloves crushed garlic

3/4 cup parmesan cheese

1/4 cup pine nuts

1/2 cup olive oil

salt and pepper to taste

Combine all ingredients in a blender. Blend until pureed. Slowly add oil while blending at low speed.

PIZZA DOUGH:

1/2 cup corn meal

1/2 cup peanut oil

3 cups unbleached flour

2 packages yeast, dissolved in
   2 cups lukewarm water

3 tablespoons olive oil

1 teaspoon salt

Mix ingredients, add 2 1/2 cups more of flour. Knead dough. Let rise 3 times.

Spread dough onto pizza pan. Brush dough with olive oil and garlic. Spread pesto sauce on pizza, top with grated mozzarella cheese and any favorite toppings (I use pepperoni, green pepper and black olives). Bake 15 minutes at 400–425°.

LINDA LOMAHAFTEWA

BECAUSE HER LIVING SPACE IN SANTA FE IS SO SMALL, THE KITCHEN TABLE PLAYS A MAJOR ROLE IN LINDA LOMAHAFTEWA'S LIFE. "I DO EVERYTHING ON THE KITCHEN TABLE—COOKING, PAINTING, SHRINKWRAPPING—EVERYTHING!" SPACE WAS NOT A PROBLEM IN THE ARTIST'S CHILDHOOD HOME, where she and her sister regularly helped her mother fix meals for a family of five. Friday night tacos, Christmas tamales, and frybread in cookie cutter shapes encouraged Lomahaftewa to enjoy and experiment with cooking.

Another carryover from childhood is her fascination with art and painting, which led her to study at the Institute of American Indian Art. Lomahaftewa obtained her MFA from San Francisco Art Institute, but she returned to Santa Fe to teach at her Alma Mater. Her favorite medium is the monoprint, and she has little trouble conveying her enthusiasm to her students. "My students come from all across the country," she says. "They keep me up to date on tribal politics and other Indian events."

Teaching also allows her to pick and choose her shows: the SWAIA Masters' show, Heard Fair and Santa Fe Indian Market. Although she makes a point of attending ceremonies in her Hopi village of Shungopavi, "I unfortunately have to miss the Snake Dance because it usually falls at the same time as Indian Market."

7

Parrot Migration

Especially when she's teaching summer classes, getting ready for "Market" can be stressful for the artist. Fortunately, her family comes to the rescue. "My Mom and Dad drive in from Phoenix to help me set up and take down my booth. My sister (who also drives in from Phoenix) and my daughter help in the booth."
Rising early and staying up late,

"I take pride in my cooking as I do with my art, and I like to experiment."

Lomahaftewa enjoys a rare treat before the show. Her mother cooks and serves the meals—provided that there's no artwork on the kitchen table!

CALIFORNIA CHILE BEANS

1 tablespoon red chile powder

1 tablespoon Schillings chili powder

1/4 cup onion (chopped)

1 clove garlic (chopped)

1 pound ground beef

2 14 oz. cans dark red
   kidney beans

1 32 oz. can stewed tomatoes
   (chopped)

In a deep frying pan, brown together meat, onion and garlic. Add spices, stewed tomatoes and kidney beans, simmer for 10 minutes. *Voila!*

Serve with corn tortillas and cheese, or fry the corn tortillas folded over with a slice of cheese, then cook until the cheese is melted.

I picked this recipe up when I was living in California. My daughter and son love this dish, as do I, it's so easy and fast to make.

JOHN GONZALES

MIT GRADUATE AND TRIBAL CONSUL-
TANT IN REGIONAL ECONOMICS, JOHN
GONZALES ONCE HAD A CHANCE FOR A
POSITION WITH THE BUSH ADMINISTRA-
TION. INSTEAD, MOTIVATED BY A REST-
LESSNESS HE COULDN'T QUITE IDENTIFY,
HE RETURNED TO HIS VILLAGE IN SAN
ILDEFONSO, NEW MEXICO. "I WANTED A
CHANGE, SOMETHING THAT PROVIDED SERENITY AND PEACE OF
MIND," HE SAYS. THEN HE BEGAN REMODELING A ROOM IN HIS
parents' home. "My dad, Lorenzo Gonzales, was a potter. He wanted a room
where he could display his work. Renovating that room got me thinking about
pottery, wondering whether I had that ability too."

While his father preferred traditional styles of pottery, Gonzales tended to
experiment. At first it seemed the two would go their separate stylistic ways;
then Gonzales asked whether he could carve one of his father's plates. "I was
surprised he said yes because I knew a lot of work went into that plate. But I
think he was sending me a message in his way."

The resulting plate was a breakthrough for Gonzales, and today "carved"
plates are his trademark. However, because he carves only the slip, and not the

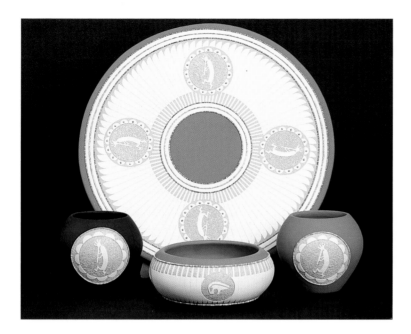

clay itself, "there's no relief surface—it's more of an etching process." Favoring ceramic stains for their deeper color, and contrasting colors within the same piece, the potter often adds turquoise or heishi borders to enhance the texture and design of the plate.

A past San Ildefonso councilman and former Chairman of the Board of the Southwestern Association for Indian Arts, Gonzales hasn't turned his back on politics completely. But in addition to his art, and with the passing of his parents, he *"Chocolate is a John Gonzales aphrodisiac."* now finds himself helping maintain the family home. His oldest son recently joined him making pots, and while he enjoys eating with his son, Gonzales does more cooking than he likes. "Everywhere I look are memories of Mom and Dad. When I cook, it's like I'm violating their space."

John's Favorite Recipe

1 can Spam Lite, cut into
  1 inch cubes
3 to 4 potatoes, peeled and sliced
1 zucchini, sliced
1 yellow squash, sliced
1 onion, sliced
1 green chile, sliced
1 tablespoon oil
salt, pepper and garlic powder
  to taste

Nuke potatoes about five minutes. Then slice potatoes, squash and onion. Place in a large skillet, with oil, over medium heat for several minutes. Add the rest of your ingredients and cook until potatoes are golden brown. Serve with warm tortillas. *Yummy!!!*

PETER B. JONES

Onondaga potter and sculptor Peter Jones made handbuilt pots and sculptures until he began experimenting with a potter's wheel. "I discovered I liked the immediate feel of wheelthrown forms," he says. "You can mold them, shape them; it's like creating your own rock to work on."

The result is what the artist calls "altered forms": effigies or clay figures with realistic hands and faces but powerfully compressed, or "altered" bodies. While Jones also works in a realistic vein, (finishing a life-size bronze for the city of Akron, Ohio in 1997), altered forms are challenging, he notes, because "you have to work fast. But when the clay shrinks, it shrinks in proportion."

An IAIA alumnus, Jones shared a studio in

Santa Fe with Doug Hyde and Kevin Redstar during the mid-seventies. It was an exciting time, he remembers, "when everyone was developing their styles. Our class had the highest number of continuing artists."

The Institute had the foresight to offer courses in "Apartment Living," the equivalent of Home Economics. "One of our tests was preparing a full course dinner for invited staff members. I also learned a lot of cooking in the IAIA when we had 'detail'," laughs Jones.

Living in New York, on the Cattaraugus reservation, Jones flies to Santa Fe for Indian Market; his sculptures, carefully placed in a trunk, are his airline baggage. His wife Roberta and daughter Lily each take a trunk, too, which they fill with hominy or Hatch's chili on the way back. His culinary tip for tourists? Denny's restaurant, which he claims still offers the best huevos rancheros. "They're not even on the menu, but if you ask for them, they'll fix 'em."

"Experiment. If it tastes good, eat it."

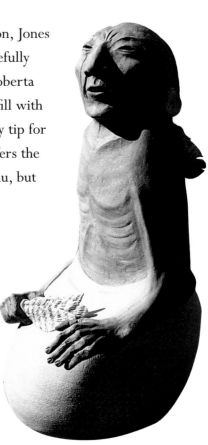

QUICK FIX POSOLE FOR CHILE ADDICTS LIVING IN NEW YORK

Cube lean pork and boil until tender. Skim fat and pork scum.

Add one can of hominy, then add one or two cans of Hatch's green chiles whole.

Add a little water and eat.

In desperation, Ortega or Old El Paso green chiles will do.

WILD ONION SOUP

Pick onions when they are about 4 to 5 inches tall. Clean by removing roots and husks.

Parboil 1/4 pound of salt pork cut into cubes.

Clean and quarter 5 or 6 medium potatoes. Boil potatoes till almost done, then add a good handful of wild onions and the pork.

Add a cup of milk, then simmer, season and serve. Season with salt and pepper to taste.

MERLIN LITTLE THUNDER

Julie and Merlin.

OCCASIONALLY, WHEN PAINTING GETS HARDER THAN USUAL, MERLIN LITTLE THUNDER THINKS ALOUD ABOUT OPENING A RESTAURANT. "MY MOTHER TAUGHT ME TO COOK. SHE WOULD GIVE ME ADVICE ON GIRLS—HOW TO COMMUNICATE WITH THEM—WHILE PEELING POTATOES, OF COURSE." THE LITTLE THUNDERS GREW UP NEAR CANTON LAKE, OKLAHOMA, on Cheyenne-Arapaho lands, where, the artist points out wryly, "We ate gourmet food and didn't even know it. We had rabbit, quail, wild greens, and wild grapes. We had teas made of tree bark and herbs. I even ate crow once because my dad always made sure we ate everything we killed."

Although his meals are a little less exotic nowadays, the artist works equally hard at preparing and presenting his food. He never shapes bread in the image of humans or animals, because "that's something Cheyennes reserve for ceremonies," he explains. When cooking, Little Thunder thinks "in colors," choosing vegetable combinations for their contrasting hues as

"IN MY FATHERS HOUSE" MERLIN LITTLE THUNDER

well as complementary tastes. A fan of Italian cuisine, he uses generous portions of garlic and olive oil in everything from "Pepper Pasta" to mashed potatoes.

As for mealtime blessings, Little Thunder explains why prayers are marathon events in Indian country. "Our belief is that the longer you pray, the longer life you'll have.

At some of our benefit dances, our old people

"There's the palette and there's the palate."

would pray almost an hour each. By the time you finally got to the food table, your legs would be hurting more than your stomach!"

GYPSY STEW

6 chicken thighs

6 Anaheim peppers, roasted,
    peeled and deseeded

3 yellow onions, quartered

8 garlic cloves

6 Roma tomatoes

10 oz. Monterey Jack cheese

In a large stock pot, place chicken, garlic and onion. Cover with water. Bring to a boil and then reduce to a simmer for about 45 minutes, or until the chicken skin is ready to be removed. Remove the skin, debone the chicken and set the meat aside.

Roast chiles and place them in a freezer bag. Put them in the freezer until almost cool, then place them in a bowl of ice water. This makes it easier to remove the skin and deseed them. Cut them into one-inch pieces.

To prepare the tomatoes, make an "x" at the top of each one with a sharp knife, then place them in a pan of boiling water for about 4 minutes. Remove the skin, quarter the tomatoes, and remove and discard the seeds.

Add everything together, except the cheese, back into the pot, like a big happy family. Let them simmer and mingle until they get to know one another real good, like a skunk scent on your leg when you get too close to ole striped back.

Cut the cheese into 1/2 inch cubes, place a few in each individual bowl, and pour hot stew over them. Be careful not to burn your mouth like my wife does. Then bon appetit!

MERLIN'S SPECIAL SALAD DRESSING AND MARINADE

6 garlic cloves, minced

4 tablespoon balsamic vinegar

3 tablespoons Worcestershire
sauce

2 tablespoons Louisiana Hot Sauce

2 tablespoons Grey Poupon
mustard

3 tablespoons olive oil

juice of three small lemons

Add to a cruet: garlic, vinegar, Worcestershire, olive oil, hot sauce. Spoon in the mustard. Last, add lemon juice and shake vigorously.

Do not refrigerate. Leave on the table or at room temperature, keeping it out of direct sunlight. *(It always gives off a rubbery taste when refrigerated.)*

Pepper Pasta with Garden Veggies and Chicken

STEP ONE

2 lbs. spaghetti or linguini

6 garlic cloves, crushed or minced

4 tablespoons olive oil

4 dry red peppers cut into thirds

1 cup dry parsley

1 bay leaf

In a cast iron skillet or frying pan, combine the garlic with 3 table-spoons of olive oil and and cook until golden brown. Remove the garlic and save it. (It has a sweet nutty taste, and is great on bread or a green salad). Add the red pepper seeds. You can add more if you like it hotter--this can be very hot! Cook until dark maroon or until it makes you cough. Oh, and I usually use 8 garlic cloves instead of 6 since we like lots of gar-lic. Remove the mixture from the heat and set it aside. Start your pasta water in a large stock pot, add 1 tablespoon of olive oil, 3 garlic cloves, sliced, 1 teaspoon of salt and 1 bay leaf. Then proceed to step two.

The pepper pasta mixture is doubled so it can be shared equally between the pasta and the garden veggies. I use the dry parsley flakes to absorb the pepper pasta mixture.

STEP TWO

4 medium carrots

2 large celery stalks

1 large white onion

15 green beans

1 medium size bell pepper

1 yellow squash

1 zucchini

2 Roma tomatoes or 6 cherry tomatoes (regular tomatoes won't work)

Prepare the garden veggies as follows:
Peel and cut up carrots into 1 inch

bite size pieces. Save any smaller pieces for the pasta water.

Cut large celery stalks into 1 inch bite size pieces. Save the tops and leaves for the pasta water.

Slice white onion into eight pieces. Save the top for the pasta water.

Cut green beans in half. Slice yellow squash and zucchini into 1/2 inch pieces. Cut Roma tomatoes into wedges, removing the seeds. Cut bell pepper into small strips. Oh, and don't forget to wash all the veggies.

Now place the carrots, onions, celery, zucchini, green beans and yellow squash in a colander. Place the colander in the boiling pasta water for one minute, then remove. This flavors and adds vitamins to the pasta water. Plus it softens the veggies a little. Now add your pasta to the boiling water and cook until *al dente*.

STEP THREE

1 lb. chicken tenders

Brown chicken in 1/2 tablespoon of pepper olive oil mixture. Don't drain. In the same frying pan, add half of the remaining oil and half the parsley. Dry all the veggies in the colander with a paper towel, then add them to the frying pan. Add Roma tomatoes and stir the mixture. Cover and cook for about 5 minutes on medium heat, then add the chicken tenders and stir together. Now add the bell pepper strips.

In a separate frying pan add the rest of the pepper oil mixture and the rest of the parsley and mix well. Let the pan get almost hot, taking care not to let the parsley get brown. Add *al dente* pasta directly from the pot with two forks. This should sizzle loudly, and as you add more pasta the sizzle calms down. Mix all this real good until the pasta is covered with the parsley mixture. Serve individually in plates, spooning the veggie and chicken mix over the pasta. Arrange as you like. Eat this while it's hot.

JACKIE SEVIER

JACKIE SEVIER WOULD NEVER HAVE
BECOME AN ARTIST IF NOT FOR HER
CHILDREN. "WHEN MY SON WAS A
BABY, HE CRIED A LOT, SO I TOOK A
DRAWING CLASS TO GET OUT IN THE
EVENINGS. I WAS OLDER AND MORE
MATURE THAN SOME OF THE OTHER
STUDENTS—I STUCK WITH IT."

Jackie and Jim Sevier

Of Northern Arapaho descent, Sevier had bead and quillworkers in her family, but no one who made a living drawing or painting. She attended college in Casper, Wyoming to compete in rodeo, and she met her husband, a professional bronc rider, there. The couple moved to Seneca, Nebraska, where both of their children have pursued rodeo. Her daughter, who graduated from college with a fine art degree, is also an artist. Now Sevier wants her to experience the practical side. "I want her to go to shows with me, so she can see how much work it is."

While she also explores pastels and mixed media compositions, Sevier's forté is embossed paper prints. Accented with gold leaf or acrylic, her paints combine contemporary form with traditional Northern Plains subject matter.

Hair Shirt (mixed media)

The embossing process involves cutting the image on a bronze plate, covering it with paper, and rolling a pressure press over it. Says the former rodeo contestant, "I have no idea how many pounds I apply because I've worn the calipers off!"

Those same arm muscles come in handy for cooking, though on a different scale than Sevier experienced as a child. "My Arapaho grandmother had a ranch at Wind River. My mother and eight aunts would do the cooking, while the men threshed grain or worked cattle. Even now, I still cook in quanity. When I fry potatoes, I cook half a sack—and there's just four of us."

"I'll eat anything that won't eat me first."

Breakfast Casserole

6 slices of bread

1 pound sausage

2 cups ham (diced)

shredded cheese (as much as you
   like and whatever kind)

1/2 cup onion (chopped)

1/2 cups green chiles

6 eggs

1/2 to 1 cup milk

1 can mushroom soup

a dab of mustard

salt and pepper to taste

Grease a 9 x 13 baking dish. Line the bottom with buttered bread slices, and then add browned and well drained sausage, diced ham, shredded cheese (as much as you like), onions, and green chiles. In a separate bowl, beat eggs, milk, mushroom soup, mustard and seasoning. Pour over the meat and bread slices.

Make sure the casserole is soggy, and bake about one hour at 350 degrees. I make several at once and freeze them.

AUNT HAZEL'S BA AC
(CHOKECHERRY GRAVY)

This recipe is from our tribe and our family. Because Aunt Hazel is the oldest of thirteen daughters, it was fitting that I ask my Auntie for her recipe.

"When the chokecherries are nice and black, wash them good until they are real mushy. Some people like crushed seeds and all, but I don't. Anyway, drain them real good in a cloth sack until you get all the juice and pulp. Bring the juice to a boil and add just a little sugar. Make a thickening of flour and water, just like you would for meat gravy. Add the thickening real slow and stir until it's the consistency you like. You can add a little more sugar if you need to.

"It tastes so good with warm fry bread or thicker as pudding."

GLOSSARY

Ba ac (Chokecherry Gravy)
Na - waw (Grandmother)
Aunt Hazel, Jackie Sevier's aunt

RUNZAS

2 packages dry yeast
1/2 cup warm water

Dissolve the yeast in warm water and let it rest while preparing the following. Make a bread mixture of:

2 cups very hot water
1/2 cup sugar
3 tablespoons real butter
1 1/2 teaspoons salt
6 to 6 1/2 cups flour

I add the yeast mixture about half-way through adding the flour. Make sure the batter is not too hot for the yeast. Knead well and let the dough rise until double.

While the yeast is rising, brown together:

2 pounds of lean hamburger
3 cups of shredded cabbage
1 small onion (diced)
seasonings and salt and pepper
   to taste

Drain well and mix in one can of cream of mushroom soup. Cube 8 oz. package of Mozarella cheese. Roll out the bread and cut into 5 inch squares. Put some meat mixture and a cheese cube on each square. Seal the edges, let rise, and bake in a shallow pan at 350 degrees until golden brown.

HOWARD SICE

SCULPTOR/JEWELER HOWARD SICE, WHO
LEARNED TO COOK FROM HIS MOM, LIKES
USING NATIVE INGREDIENTS LIKE PIÑON
AND CILANTRO IN HIS COOKING. "BUT,"
HE LAUGHS, "MY WIFE, PATRICIA, DOESN'T
LIKE ME TO COOK TOO MUCH BECAUSE I
USE EVERY POT IN THE HOUSE!"

THE FORMER TOXICOLOGIST FIRST BECAME INTERESTED IN
JEWELRY-MAKING WHILE DOING SIZING AND REPAIR WORK IN HIS
spare time. Then his Navajo father-in law literally passed him the torch—and
file—encouraging him to take up jewelry as an occupation, not a hobby. But it was
cowboy artist Yelles Newman who pointed Sice towards his specialty by showing
him elaborately engraved belt buckles. "You don't see anyone doing engraving
with Indian designs," Newman told him. So the Hopi/Laguna jeweler set to work.

"Imagine a Navajo rug on a belt buckle—that's what I do," says Sice. "It's a
technique that leaves little room for error because you're carving metal. If you
goof up, you have to make the same mistake all the way around!"

An Arizona resident, Sice works on a large scale as well, designing functional

metal art and furniture, even playground equipment like his Mimbres cater-
pillar tunnel. A recent art project for the Phoenix Art Commission involved
designing and cutting copper medallions (100 in all) to hang from lamp posts
on Central Avenue.

Currently exploring the Internet in marketing his large works, Sice explains
that his wife does his quality control. "She points out where my mistakes are, or
where something needs polish-
ing." Even his mother helps, *I haven't met a meal I didn't like. . . yet!*
making sure the couple is well
provisioned at art shows. Says Sice, "She's in her mid-seventies and she's still
making oven bread for our trips!"

PARAJE'S DELUXE SANGWICH

a loaf of oven bread, made in
   Pueblo beehive oven
yellow stuff (mustard)
rabbit food (lettuce)
reservation round steak
   (bologna)
Kool-Aid (red)

This recipe was passed on to me by my Uncle Roy.

Take the ceremonial bread knife from the sacred knife drawer in the kitchen (you know it's sacred because your mother won't let you in there if she's home).

Cut the loaf into half inch slices. Place a slice of reservation steak on the bread, spread the yellow stuff all over the steak, add the rabbit food on top of the steak. Place a final slice of bread on top.

Serve cold with red Kool-Aid under a shady tree.

Thanks, Uncle Roy!
Bon Appetit!

P.S. For the adventurous, fry the bologna.

HOWIE'S COOKOUT

steak, preferably one inch thick
   (pork chops will do)
1/4 cup dried red chile
1/4 cup shelled piñons
1/2 stick butter or margarine
1/4 cup fresh cilantro
   (chopped fine)
hot barbecue grill

Slice steak down the center lengthwise to form a pocket.
 Mix piñons, chile and cilantro and heat with butter in a saucepan until a paste forms. Remove from stove and place all of the mixture inside the steak. Place the steak on a grill and cook to desired doneness.

Serve with wild rice and red wine or red Kool-Aid

FOR DESSERT

One warm tortilla (thick, home-made) with commodity grape jelly

OR:

(my favorite)
Plain sugar sprinkled on a hot tortilla

DAVID GAUSSOIN

WHEN DAVID GAUSSOIN WENT TO ITALY, HE SAW MONUMENTAL PAINTINGS AND SCULPTURE. BUT HE ALSO SPENT A LOT OF TIME LOOKING AT JEWELRY--NOT ADMIRING A PARTICULAR BRACELET OR NECKLACE, BUT EXAMINING CLASPS AND FINDINGS. "A JEWELER'S VIEWPOINT IS DIFFERENT. YOU'RE ALWAYS LOOKING AT HOW THINGS ARE PUT TOGETHER," HE LAUGHS.

Son of jeweler Connie Gaussoin, David was a biology major at the University of New Mexico until he realized that marketing was a better fit. He balances academics with jewelry making, which has a special place in his heart. "I've been making jewelry since I was twelve. It was my way of expressing myself. When I was little, watching my mother work, I'd ask, 'Can I play too?'"

Like his mother, Gaussoin used traditional Navajo technique, cutting his jewelry molds from the porous volcanic rock as tufa. It's a complicated, unpredictable process, but "it has a spiritual quality," he observes. "It's not like prefabricated work. Everything has to go right for tufa casting to come out."

Although he uses a traditional casting process, the Navajo/Picuris jeweler tries to be innovative with designs and materials. His trip to Italy, for example, inspired a cross-shaped necklace with a strand of apricot-colored freshwater pearls.

Sharing a transformed garage/studio with his mother which they jokingly call "the sweatshop," David cultivates a garden in the summer because he likes being outdoors. He likes

"As your tastes change, so does your food—and your art."

to cook in a healthy style— "Chinese rice or pasta and lots of salads." That's something else he admires about Italy—the quality of the food, sold in open air markets. "It's a lot fresher, easier to digest. I wish we could get that here," he remarks.

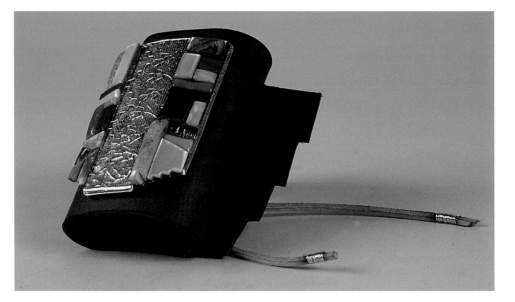

DAVE'S QUICK AND EASY SALSA

1 small can stewed tomatoes

3-4 tablespoons picante sauce
   (I like it hot)

dash of garlic salt and pepper
   to taste

1 lime cut into wedges

Place tomatoes into blender, add picante to taste, garlic salt (the more garlic salt, the better the salsa), and a dash of pepper to taste. Blend quickly, just enough to chop the tomatoes to a nice chunky size.

Pour salsa into a bowl, squeeze in lime juice and stir.

Serve with blue corn tortilla chips and enjoy!!

This is the quickest snack to prepare. Just have fun with it, and add or delete to taste.

MEL CORNSHUCKER

Mel and his daughter Morgan

WHEN MEL CORNSHUCKER BREAKS
A BOWL OR A CUP, HE DOESN'T
WORRY. HE CAN ALWAYS PUT
ANOTHER IN THE KILN. THE
CHEROKEE POTTER, WHO STARTED
HIS CAREER MAKING VASES, SOON
DISCOVERED THAT HIS FAVORITE PART OF THE PROCESS WAS DECO-
RATING THEM. THAT'S WHEN HE SWITCHED TO DISHWARE, HAND-
PAINTING HIS CREATIONS WITH designs like dragonfly, turtle and
Kokopelli. "I wanted more surfaces to paint on," he explains. "Pie plates,
bowls and casseroles give you more surfaces."

Finished with homey blue and brown glazes, Cornshucker's stoneware recalls
comfort foods he ate as a boy on his grandmother's farm. Every weekend, the
family, who lived in Kansas City, Missouri, would drive to her farm in Jay,
Oklahoma, and the cooking ritual would begin. "My grandma would go out
Saturday morning, kill a chicken, and bake it in a dutch oven on Sunday. Then
we'd go to church, and when we got back we'd have chicken and homemade
angel food cake."

Even then, Cornshucker was fascinated by the transforming powers of an oven, teaching himself to bake cookies and cakes. He's kept his sweet tooth, but now he gravitates towards main courses like casseroles, the shape of a dish often inspiring his choice of ingredients.

Though not all his creations are food-oriented, the popularity of one utilitarian dish, his "buffalo bowl," proved almost too much for the potter. It attracted the attention of a catalog company, which put him on contract to produce the bowl in quantity. The first month, orders to his Missouri studio were manageable. But by the second month, they had risen to a hundred bowls a week—with backorders! "After a year, I had to quit. I got too tired," admits Cornshucker, "but I bought a Carman Ghia and upgraded my shop, so it was worth it!"

"Food . . . it got me where I am today."

RICE CASSEROLE

1 cup cooked regular rice, cold

3 eggs, separated

2 tablespoon melted butter or
   margarine

1/2 cup milk

salt to taste

1 cup cheddar cheese, shredded

paprika

Combine rice, egg yolks, butter, milk, salt and cheese. Mix well. Beat egg whites until stiff, fold into rice mixture. Pour into a lightly greased 1 quart casserole or soufflé dish. Sprinkle with paprika.

Bake, uncovered, at 325 degrees for 30-40 minutes or until firm and golden brown.

Yield: 2 to 4 servings.

BROCCOLI SALAD

2 to 3 bunches broccoli

1 small onion, chopped

1/2 cup raisins

1/2 cup sunflower seeds

3/4 cup bacon, cooked, and
   crumbled (add last)

DRESSING:

1 cup mayonnaise

1/2 cup sugar

1 1/2 tablespoons vinegar

Mix well and add to the salad.

BREAD PUDDING

softened butter or margarine

6 slices white bread

4 eggs

1 cup sugar, divided

1 teaspoon vanilla extract

dash of salt

3 cups of milk

1 teaspoon ground cinnamon

1 8 oz. package cream cheese,
   softened

Butter the bread and cut it into 1 inch squares. Place it in a lightly greased 11 3/4" X 7 1/2" X 1 3/4" baking dish.

Slightly beat 3 eggs. Add 1/2 cup sugar, vanilla and salt; mix well. Pour over bread squares; sprinkle with cinnamon.

Combine cream cheese and 1/2 cup sugar, blend until smooth. Add one egg, beating well. Spread the mixture evenly over the soaked bread. Bake at 350 degrees for 45 minutes or until firm. Cool slightly.

Yields: 8 servings.

CHICKEN ENCHILADAS

2 cups cooked, chopped chicken

2 cans green chile enchilada sauce

1/2 cup chopped onion

4 oz. can chopped green chiles

2 small cartons of whipping cream

3/4 teaspoon salt

1 cup shredded jack cheese

black olives to taste

8 tortillas (corn or flour)

Mix cooked, chopped chicken, enchilada sauce, onion and green chiles. Mix whipping cream into salt. Dip each tortilla into whipping cream, then place the sauce mixture into each tortilla and roll. Place in a lightly greased baking dish. Pour the rest of the whipping cream over the enchiladas. Top with cheese and sprinkle with olives. Cover and bake at 350 degrees for 25 minutes.

BILL GLASS, JR.

RAISED IN ARIZONA AND NEW MEXICO, OKLAHOMA POTTER BILL GLASS, JR. ENCOUNTERED A VARIETY OF FOODS. "MY FATHER WORKED FOR THE BUREAU OF INDIAN AFFAIRS, SO WE WERE EXPOSED TO ALL KINDS OF COOKING—MUTTON STEW, REAL MEXICAN FOOD—IT MADE ME WILLING TO TRY NEW THINGS."

WHEREVER THE CHEROKEE FAMILY WENT, THEY ALSO PUT IN A GARDEN, EVEN WHEN IT MEANT HAULING IN SOIL FROM THE MOUNTAINS. "THERE WERE two places we didn't have much luck, Flagstaff and Tohatchi. We grew a few salad items--lettuce, carrots, tomatoes—but that's about it."

Now back in northeastern Oklahoma, the award-winning ceramicist still gardens a little but cooks (i.e. microwaves) only when he has to. "I'm the taste-tester of the family. My wife, Connie, is head cook for Locust Grove Middle

School— so she tries out her recipes on me," he explains.

One thing Connie doesn't do is prepare or serve food in her husband's richly glazed pots. Covered with ancient southeastern motifs like the Serpent and Sun symbols, his pots are purely aesthetic, meant for display only. Along with his ceramic busts and sculptures, they have pro- *"Try not to laugh or sneeze while eating piki."* pelled his recognition as one of the Five Tribes' "Master Artists." Glass carefully plans design areas on his works, to guide the viewer's eye from one spot to another. "I try to create movement with color and design, movement that follows the shape of the pot."

Bill's favorite cooks are his mother and his wife; his idea of a good meal is wild onions, beans and cornbread. His best travel memories revolve around the reunions the Glass family had on the Illinois river each summer. "We'd camp and swim and fish. It seems like everything always tasted better down on the river."

MOM'S FRIED PIES

2 cups self rising flour

1/3 cup shortening

3/4 cup milk

14 oz. fruit pie filling (apple, cherry etc.)

Cut shortening into flour and add milk. Mix well.

Roll crust out onto a floured board. Pinch off enough to cover a saucer. Place approximately 3 tablespoons of cold pie filling on half of the crust, then fold and crimp the edges. Puncture the crust with a fork to allow steam to escape. Deep fry in shortening.

PRACHA'S (TOMMY'S) THAI CURRY

2-3 pound roast (sliced thin)

1 tablespoon curry powder

2 teaspoons garlic powder

16 oz. fresh mushrooms (sliced)

3 tablespoons soy sauce

8 oz. can of sliced bamboo shoots (drained)

2   8 oz. cans of sliced water chestnuts (drained)

2   12 oz. cans Milnot Milk

1 jalapeno (chopped)

salt to taste

3 cups water

Brown meat in a lightly oiled skillet. Add curry, garlic powder, mushrooms and water, and simmer 30 minutes (add water if needed). Add soy, bamboo shoots and water chestnuts, then continue simmering 10-20 minutes. Add Milnot, jalapenos and salt, and cook approximately 10 more minutes.

Garnish with green pepper strips, and serve over rice. We like to top it with picante sauce.

JANE OSTI

MIXING GLAZES FOR HER HAR-
VEST OF CLAY AND RAKU POTS,
JANE OSTI MEASURES HER
INGREDIENTS WITH A CHEMIST'S
SCALE—IN GRAMS. BUT WHEN IT
COMES TO COOKING, SHE GOES BY SIGHT AND SPRINKLES, LIKE
HER AUNT DELLA.

"My mother died when I was five and my Aunt Della raised me and my
sister. She never owned a measuring cup or spoon, but her baking was unparal-
leled." Riding home on the school bus, Osti remembers stepping out onto the
dirt road and being met by the open-armed smell of baking cinnamon rolls.

Her aunt introduced her to wild foods, too—wild onions, greens and
watercress—gathered in the woods by their house. Osti (whose Italian sur-
name by marriage sounds like her Cherokee nickname, "usti," or "little"), has
fond memories of her gathering treks along the creek. "We ate everything that
came up in the spring. I think those wild foods made us strong."

Indeed, without stamina the potter could never maintain her rigorous schedule of art shows, studio work, and classes conducted in her Pryor, Oklahoma home. A vegetarian since the 1970's, Osti builds her diet around "high energy foods" like yogurt, fruit and salad. About all she cooks today is pots—bodacious yet elegant vessels incised with ancient criss-cross designs and scroll patterns. After all, wood is a fuel she knows well. "I was in the fourth grade before my aunt gave up her wood stove," she laughs.

"How you feel affects the food you prepare. It needs to be done with love."

Hearty Oatmeal Cake

1 1/4 cups boiling water
1 cup oats

Combine and let stand one hour.

CREAM TOGETHER:
1/2 cup butter or margarine
1 cup sugar
1 cup brown sugar
2 eggs

ADD:
1 1/3 cups flour
1 teaspoon cinnamon
1 teaspoon baking soda
oats

Mix well and bake at 350 degrees for 45 minutes.

TOPPING:
3 tablespoons butter
2/3 cups sugar
1 cup coconut
1 cup nuts (optional)
2 egg yolks
4 tablespoons milk
1/2 teaspoon vanilla

Combine in a saucepan and heat approximately 10 minutes, stirring continuously. Top the cake after it has cooled.

Carrot Cake Supreme

1 1/2 cups corn oil

2 cups sugar

3 eggs

2 cups flour

2 teaspoons cinnamon

2 teaspoons baking soda

2 teaspoons vanilla

1/2 teaspoon salt

3 cups peeled shredded carrots

1 cup pecans

1/2 cup crushed pineapple

Mix all ingredients until well blended. Bake in a greased and floured 3 quart baking pan at 350 degrees for 60 minutes. (Reduce heat 25 degrees if using a glass dish.)

FROSTING:

1/2 cup butter or margarine

8 oz. cream cheese

1 box confectioners sugar

1 teaspoon vanilla

1 cup pecans (optional)

Cream together all ingredients. Ice the cake after it has cooled.

JANE'S APPLE FOOD CAKE

2 cups sugar

2 sticks butter or margarine

2 eggs

2 1/4 cups flour

1 teaspoon vanilla

1 cup pecans (optional)

2 teaspoons baking soda

1 teaspoon cinnamon

1 teaspoon nutmeg

1/4 teaspoon ground cloves

4 cups diced and peeled apples

1 cup crushed pineapple

Cream together: sugar, butter and eggs.

Mix dry ingredients and sift into butter mixture. Add apples, nuts and vanilla.

Bake in greased and floured 3 quart baking pan at 350 degrees for 45 minutes or until cooked through. (Reduce heat 25 degrees if using a glass dish.)

FERNANDO PADILLA

PAINTER FERNANDO PADILLA PRIDES HIMSELF ON SPICY GREEN CHILI STEW. UNFORTUNATELY, HE CAN NEVER MAKE IT HOT ENOUGH—BUT NOT FOR LACK OF INGREDIENTS. HE TRAVELS REGULARLY FROM OKLAHOMA CITY TO NEW MEXICO FOR CHILIS. "THE PROBLEM IS, NOBODY IN MY HOUSE LIKES THEIR CHILI AS HOT AS I DO," HE SMILES.

Padilla, who was raised in San Felipe Pueblo, paints oils and acrylics of Southwestern landscape and Pueblo life. But he carefully screens his images. "My village doesn't allow drawing or sketching," he explains. "I change scenery and other details in my painting so I'm not precisely reproducing anything."

Keeping to tradition has always beeen important to Padilla, who by fourth grade had learned from his mother how to make flour tortillas and frybread. His father, who cooked at a number of Indian schools, frequently tried his hand at more exotic fare: shrimp dinners, for example. Although Padilla was often reluctant to try his father's dishes, as an adult he learned to appreciate variety and to experiment with recipes himself. On a recent trip to Germany to market

Walpi

his art, he sampled all kinds of food, from German to Italian to Greek.

After his return to the States, Padilla was commissioned to paint a mural for the Denver International Airport. The artist had never attempted anything that large. He thought back to murals he'd seen in Germany by his favorite painter, Rubens, and indulged in a moment of wishful thinking: "Rubens had a huge school of students working for him, enlarging his drawings, blocking in his color. Then he came in and touched it up."

"Looking in the pantry and conceiving new and spontaneous recipes is a challenge I enjoy."

GREEN CHILE STEW

1 1/2 lbs. lean pork, round steak
    or a mixture of both, cut into
    1/2 inch cubes
cooking oil
1 medium onion, chopped
4 cups water
4 medium potatoes, cubed
3 large garlic cloves, minced
2 teaspoons salt
1/3 teaspoon pepper
1 lb. green chiles, chopped
2 medium tomatoes, cubed

In a large saucepan, over medium heat, brown meat in a little oil, stirring frequently. Be sure the meat is well browned. Add chopped onion and continue browning for 5 minutes. Add water, potatoes, and fast simmer for 15 minutes, or until the potatoes are done. Add green chiles, tomatoes, garlic, salt and pepper. Continue to simmer for 10 minutes, stirring frequently.

Makes 2 quarts.

PUEBLO OVEN BREAD

9 cups flour

2 packages dry yeast

2 teaspoons salt

2 1/2 cups warm water

5 tablespoon lard or oil

In a large bowl, mix yeast and 1/2 cup warm water Stir in melted lard or oil and add salt. Then add portions of flour and water alternately and knead the mixture until it is smooth and elastic. Place a ball of dough in a large oiled bowl and cover it with a damp cloth. Let it rise for several hours, or until double in bulk. Punch down and knead well. Divide into 4 balls, then place them in oil-lined round pans. Let them rise again. Bake for 50-60 minutes in a 400 degree oven until brown on top. Traditionally, the loaves are baked in an outdoor adobe oven.

SCOTT FRAZIER

Scott and Marsha Frazier

W HEN WOLVES WERE REINTRO-
DUCED IN YELLOWSTONE PARK IN
1995, SCOTT FRAZIER AND HIS
WIFE MARSHA GAVE THE NATIVE
AMERICAN BLESSING. IT WAS AN
EMOTIONAL MOMENT FOR FRAZIER.
"IT HAS TO DO WITH FREEDOM," HE SAYS. "INDIAN PEOPLE WERE
PUT ON RESERVATIONS AND BROUGHT UP WITH PEOPLE LOOKING AT
us through cages, too." The Fraziers were so powerfully affected by the moment
that they vowed to return and perform a Sun Dance, which they did in 1997.

Frazier and his wife live in Bozeman, Montana, where they run a non-profit
corporation that emphasizes ceremonial cultural education. But the Santee
Sioux/Crow artist is best known for making traditional dolls, cultural emmis-
aries in their own right.

Shortly after he was injured in an oil refinery accident, Frazier started
experimenting with doll-making as part of his physical rehabilitation program.
Using an old family doll as a model, he cut a body from suede and made an outfit for it. Though he didn't realize it at the time, Frazier was among the first
Indian artists to revive the traditional "no face" dolls and turn them into an art
form. He and Marsha do extensive research on outfits for the dolls, "but we've

Antelope Santee Dolls

copied one. We feel that's intrusive—we don't want to violate clan customs."

Frazier is a self-taught cook, although he now jokes that these days, "I'm the exalted one, who waits for the food to arrive." With their multiple businesses, the Fraziers find little time to cook, relying on their crockpot for meals—"We make a lot of stews and soups in the fall."

"As I eat candy, the smile of something sweet goes into my dolls, so they are not made from anger."

Frazier approaches his dolls thoughtfully, eating candy while he works, to create good feelings "so they're not made from anger." And his outfits never include weapons. "I don't want aggression," he says. "I have this suspicion that if I give them a weapon, they'll sneak one into a cat."

ANTELOPE SEA JUBILEE

1 cup vegetable or chicken stock

1 inch chunk fresh ginger root

2 tablespoons soy sauce

2 tablespoons cornstarch

Put the stock in a bowl and grate ginger into the stock. Grate until you hit the the hard middle. Add soy sauce and set aside.

half a salmon

8 large shrimp, shelled

MARINATE THESE IN:

3 tablespoons soy sauce

1 teaspoon brown sugar

1 large clove garlic, pressed into the soy sauce

Mix all three ingredients together and pour over the salmon and shrimp—refrigerate two hours.

   Grill the salmon and shrimp (broiling will do).

VEGGIE MEDLEY

CHOP TOGETHER:

1 sweet red pepper

small bunch scallions

8 large mushrooms

8 spears asparagus or broccoli heads

2 chopped marinated artichoke hearts

Sauté the veggie medley in a table-spoon of olive oil or steam in steamer (if you like crunchy veggies, sauté; if soft, steam).

Recipe continued on page 54.

1 small package angel hair pasta
   Boil to directions on package.
Rinse and set aside, covered in
   steam.

Chop assorted salad greens and set aside.

Chop 2 ripe Roma tomatoes and set aside.

Mix cornstarch with the cooled stock mixture and bring to a boil until it forms a loose gravy, stirring constantly. Do not let the mixture get too thick.

SERVE IN LARGE PASTA BOWLS:

Line the bowls with salad greens, add warm pasta, then veggie medley, then salmon and shrimp, pour gravy over the top and garnish with tomatoes! Then you are ready to eat and have a doll show!

ANTELOPE BUFFALO STEW

1 lb. buffalo hamburger or
    stew meat
2 cups chicken broth
1 cup posole or hominy
1 onion, chopped
12 wild turnips, halved
1 small bag baby carrots
2 cups water

Slow cook in a big pot all day, or cook fast in a pressure cooker for 25 minutes.

FRY BREAD—GRANDMOTHER FRAZIER'S OLD RECIPE

2 cups flour
2 teaspoons baking powder
1/2 teaspoon salt
3/4 cup milk

Sift flour, baking powder and salt together. Add milk gradually until the mixture is soft. Turn out on a slightly flared board. Pat out about 1/2 inch thick and cut into desired shapes. Slash a slit in the center, deep fry in hot Crisco.

Serve stew and fry bread together and be ready for second requests!

Amado Peña

AMADO PEÑA IS KNOWN FOR
GENEROUS SUPPORT OF GOOD
CAUSES. BUT THESE DAYS, HE
WEARS HIS ART, AS WELL AS
HIS HEART, ON HIS SLEEVE.
THE SANTA FE-BASED ARTIST RECENTLY BROUGHT OUT A LINE OF
MEN'S AND WOMEN'S CLOTHING, INCLUDING ACCESSORIES LIKE
NECKTIES AND SILK SCARVES.

Marketed to select western-wear stores and boutiques, Peña's fabric designs
reflect his trademark blend of Indian and Hispanic cultures. They hearken back
to the days when "Southwest art" was partly synonymous with his renderings of
angular men and women in serapes, blankets and mantas. So popular were his
stylized serigraphs, paintings and prints that the Yaqui/Hispanic artist had his
own gallery. Although he sold the gallery at one point to concentrate on originals, Peña has now reopened it. A new addition is a wine-tasting room featuring
a line of vintages with Peña-designed bottle labels.

He and his wife, JB, a weaver herself and owner of "Handwoven Originals"
in Santa Fe, share studio space at their ranch in Nambé. When it comes to

kitchen work, however, JB reigns supreme. "I'm the gofer," laughs Peña. "My mother tried to teach me to cook, but I wasn't a very good student. I learned just enough to survive my many years of bachelorhood."

What he preferred instead was hunting deer, javelina and quail at the family ranch, thirty-eight miles north of Laredo. The ranch was a favorite meeting place for holidays and family reunions. And javelina, as it turns out, makes great tamales. "Every December, my grandmother, mother and other relatives would make two or three hundred tamales. And we'd still be eating them in March."

"If it doesn't walk off the plate, we can be friends."

AMADO'S MIGAS

1 tablespoon olive oil

1/2 onion (chopped)

2 cloves garlic (chopped)

1 dozen corn tortillas (cut into strips, may substitute Doritos)

6 eggs

1/4 cup milk

1/2 cup Monterey Jack or Cheddar cheese (shredded)

fresh roasted red or green chiles (chopped), or salsa to taste

handful of fresh chopped cilantro

mushrooms (optional)

In a large skillet, sauté onion and garlic in oil, browning the mixture. Add tortillas and fry until slightly crisp. In a separate bowl, combine eggs and milk, add to the onion mixture, and continue to cook, stirring slowly to allow the eggs to finish. Add cheese and mushrooms, and stir in chiles or salsa to taste. Garnish with fresh chopped cilantro. Molé sauce may be substituted for chiles or salsa.

FREETO PIE

1 can pinto beans

1 pound ground turkey

red chile powder (season to taste)

1 medium onion (chopped)

Cheddar cheese (shredded)

10 oz. bag of Fritos

Brown meat and onion to a sizzle. Add cooked beans with juice and season with red chile powder to taste. In a casserole dish or in individual serving bowls, layer Fritos, meat mixture and cheese. Heat and serve.

SANDRA AND MICHAEL HORSE

SANDRA AND MICHAEL HORSE ARE A RARITY— A COUPLE THAT MOVES BACK AND FORTH FROM THE PERFORMING ARTS TO JEWELRY. MICHAEL, OF YAQUI/ZUNI/MESCALERO APACHE DESCENT, SPENDS MUCH OF HIS TIME ACTING FOR TV AND FILM. AMONG HIS CREDITS IS THE CANADIAN TV SERIES "NORTH OF 60." BUT HE IS ALSO ARTIST-IN-RESIDENCE AT THE SOUTHWEST MUSEUM IN LOS ANGELES. IN ADDITION TO PAINTING AND MAKING traditional items, he draws upon his Zuni heritage for high-color and often humorous silver and inlay jewelry.

Sandra's jewelry also has a Southwest flavor, which she credits to her husband. Although she approaches other elements of her life with considerable strength and self-assertion, she expresses surprise that her jewelry "comes out looking so feminine and graceful." She associates her love of filigree with the floral motifs of her Cree heritage and her fondness for freshwater pearls with her Japanese ancestry.

Sandra's jewelry has a feminine touch . . .

Like their jewelry, the couple's cooking styles are diverse. Michael, who doesn't like to cook for fewer than ten people, uses South-western touches like piñon nuts, cilantro and chili in much of his cooking. "My wife doesn't like hot food, so when she cooks for me, I cover everything with salsa," he explains.

A fan of comfort foods—pork chops, creamed corn, mashed potatoes, Sandra specializes in desserts. "I believe people have two stomachs," she says, "the food stomach and the dessert stomach. Which is why, no matter how much you eat, you always have room for dessert."

Living in North Hollywood, California, both partners work hard to balance their home life, relationship and careers. A recent radio play gave the couple a

chance to perform together at the Gene Autry Museum. And there's always an LA restaurant to take in. Michael notes that one of his friends who owns a restaurant offers 'celebrity burgers' on his menu." I tried to convince him to name one after me," he quips, "but he didn't think the 'Horseburger' would be a very good seller."

"Food should be prepared while listening to your favorite music."
—*Michael*

"People have two stomachs—the food stomach and the dessert stomach. Food can never enter the dessert stomach, so no matter how much food you've eaten, there's always room for dessert."
—*Sandra*

. . . while Michael's is very masculine.

GRILLED POLENTA FINGERS WITH ROASTED RED PEPPER SAUCE

1/2 cup chicken broth

1 teaspoon olive oil

1/2 cup yellow cornmeal or quick
   cooking polenta

1 cup water

In large, heavy-bottomed saucepan, bring water and chicken broth to a boil. Add salt if needed.

Gradually add cornmeal in a thin stream, whisking constantly. Reduce heat to medium and stir gently with a wooden spoon, until polenta becomes solid and pulls away from the side of the pan, about 20 minutes. (Quick cooking will be about 8 minutes, or follow package instructions.) Remove from heat and let stand until cooled to room temperature, about 5 minutes.

Shape cooled polenta into three long loaves. Cover with plastic wrap and refrigerate until firm. This can be done 1-3 days ahead of time.

TO SERVE:

Slice chilled polenta into eight long, slim fingers. Place a non-stick saucepan over medium heat for 30 seconds. Add oil, heat 30 seconds more. Add polenta and cook, turning occasionally, until crisp and shiny on all sides, about 6-8 minutes.

Serve immediately with Roasted Red Pepper Sauce.

Serves 2

Roasted Red Pepper Sauce

4 medium red bell peppers

2 small garlic cloves, crushed*

1/4 cup chicken stock broth

1 medium onion, sliced

2 teaspoons olive oil

1 tablespoon red wine vinegar

Peppers may be prepared one of three different ways—grilled on a barbecue until blackened, baked on a foil-lined cookie sheet for 45 minutes at 375 degrees until blackened, or flame-broiled very carefully over an open stove until blackened.

Place hot blackened peppers into a plastic bag and seal. Let them steam a few minutes, and rub the peppers through the bag until the blackened skin is removed. Do not put them under water, as this will wash away the flavor. Core, de-seed and chop the peppers.

Place peppers in a baking dish, add garlic, onion and olive oil. Roast in the oven for 25 minutes. Add broth. Cover with foil and bake 20 minutes. Allow to cool, then add vinegar. Purée in a blender until smooth.

Pour the sauce over polenta fingers. Top with arugula and grated or shaved parmesan cheese. The sauce is also great over pasta or cold chicken salad.

For a sweeter, nuttier garlic flavor, remove the outer skin of the garlic heads, leaving the cloves intact. Slice off the top portion of the head to expose individual cloves. Sprinkle lightly with olive oil. Wrap in foil. Bake in the oven at 350 degrees for 45-60 minutes or until the cloves are soft. Squeeze out the garlic and add it to the last 20 minutes in the oven. The garlic can also be cooked on a barbecue. The garlic paste alone is great as a spread on bread.

BILL PROKOPIOF

NATIVE PEOPLES HAVE ALWAYS KNOWN THAT
ART HAS A SPIRIT. BUT BILL PROKOPIOF'S
SCULPTURES SEEM TO HAVE A GOOD TIME AS
WELL. THE NEW MEXICO SCULPTOR CON-
FESSES THAT HE WORKS BEST WHEN HE'S
HAPPY. "AND I'M HAPPY WHEN I'M WELL
FED," HE ADDS.

Of Alaskan Aleut ancestry, Prokopiof retains his love of fish, which has not
diminished since he moved inland. Hence his recipe for "Peru Fish Pie," bor-
rowed from his sister Rosie and salmon steaks which he prepares on an outdoor grill. When it comes to meat, however, Prokopiof's tastes have always
been those of a flatlander. "I got teased about that," he recalls. "Like the time I
came home for lunch—I was about eleven or twelve—and there was this gor-
geous smell in the kitchen. Then my mother brought this baked seal out of the
oven. And I don't do seal meat."

A graduate of the Institute of American Indian Art, Prokopiof now parti-
cipates in the school's Masters Program. The program arranges yearly exhibitions
for its members, giving Prokopiof a chance to indulge one of his favorite

"A happy artist does happy work."

habits: eating out.
Sometimes that's
all it takes to make a
dead show bearable, like
the one that opened in a
Soho gallery on a bitterly
cold Super Bowl Sunday. Few
collectors came in during the run of
the show, but some New York friends
rescued the artist. "Every night, after
the show, they'd take me to a good
restaurant."

BILL'S FAVORITE PERU (FISH PIE)

pie crust for a 9 x 13 oblong pan
   (enough for bottom and top)
4 cups long grain white rice,
   cooked
1 cup onions, diced
4 hard boiled eggs, sliced
3 to 5 lbs. fresh halibut, cod or
   salmon, sliced
salt and pepper to taste

Line the pan with pie crust. Layer the ingredients, starting with rice, followed by the onion, salt and pepper, fish slices, egg slices and a final layer of rice. Cover with pie crust, crimp edges together, and vent the crust by slitting holes on top. Brush the top crust with milk. Bake 45-60 minutes at 400 degrees. Cut in squares and serve with lemon wedges and butter. Best served hot, but also makes great leftovers.

This particular dish is always made in my honor whenever I visit my relatives in Seattle. Mom always knows what to serve to make it all better!

ROBERT MONTOYA

"PUEBLO INDIANS NEVER COUNT THE LOAVES OF BREAD THEY MAKE BECAUSE COUNTING ONLY ENSURES YOU WON'T HAVE ENOUGH," SAYS PAINTER ROBERT MONTOYA. A FORMER CITY PLANNER, MONTOYA FIRST BEGAN PAINTING IN 1970, EVOLVING HIS OWN ABSTRACT VISUAL LANGUAGE TO DEPICT PUEBLO CEREMONIALISM, LEGENDS AND STORIES.

From San Juan and Sandia Pueblos, Montoya grew up eating venison, elk bone stew, rabbit, quail and fish, along with fruits and vegetables his family raised. The painter helped his grandfather and cousins hoe, weed and irrigate the fields. "Everything was done by hand. Those were beautiful, hard-working days, from sunup to sunset."

Now working for the federal government, Montoya lives in Albuquerque. His

"All families should eat at least one meal together ervery day—even it's just leftovers."

Prayers of the Rain Makers

evenings and weekends are spent painting with casein, his primary medium. "Discipline is the key, telling yourself it has to get done. No one will do it for you."

In his spare time, Montoya enjoys fixing Pueblo dishes such as red and green chili or squash and Mexican food like his red chili cheese enchilada casserole. Food and drink, however, are strictly forbidden in his work area. "I learned that lesson early on when I spilled coffee on a painting," he laughs.

Bob's Picnic or Camp Beans

1 large slice of pre-cooked ham
   (diced to 1/2 inch cubes)
8 slices smoked bacon
1 Polish Kielbasa sausage (cut in
   1/4 inch slices)
1 15oz. can butter beans
1 15 oz. can navy beans
1 15 oz. can kidney beans
1 15 oz. can pork and beans
1/2 onion (diced)
1 1/2 cups brown sugar
1/2 cup barbecue sauce

Brown bacon and onions together and drain thoroughly. Add ham and sausage, and brown slightly. Drain all beans of most liquid, with the exception of the pork and beans. Add the beans, sugar, and barbecue sauce, and simmer 5 to 10 minutes.

GREEN CHILE FRITO PIE

1 to 1 1/2 lbs. coarse ground beef
   or pork
4 cups diced green chiles
   (medium or hot)
4 cloves garlic (diced)
1 teaspoon ground pepper
1 tablespoon salt or to taste
   (remember, the chips and
   cheese are salty)
Velveeta cheese
Fritos
3 to 4 cups water

Brown meat and drain thoroughly. Add water, salt, pepper, garlic, and green chile, then bring to a low simmer. Simmer 5 to 10 minutes or until all flavors interact.

Place a handful of Fritos in a soup bowl, add a slice of Velveeta cheese, and spoon the green chile mixture over them. Fantastic on a cold winter day.

CHILE STEW

1 1/2 lbs. coarse ground beef or
pork

4 cups diced green chiles
(medium or hot)

4 cloves garlic (diced)

2 tablespoons salt

1 tablespoon ground pepper

1/2 onion (chopped)

5 small to medium potatoes
(cubed, bite size)

3 ears corn (cut from cob) or
a 12 oz. can whole kernel corn

2 medium size zucchini (cubed,
bite size)

2 medium size yellow squash
(cubed, bite size)

4 to 6 cups water (depending
on preferred consistency)

Brown the meat in a stew pot and drain thoroughly. Add garlic, onions, chile, salt, pepper, and water, then bring to a low simmer. Add diced potatoes and simmer 5 to 10 minutes or until potatoes soften somewhat. Do not get potatoes mushy.

Add the corn, squash, and zucchini, then simmer another 5 minutes or until the the squash and zucchini soften.

This version can be modified to the vegetarian taste by eliminating the meat.

DENNY HASKEW

TRACING HIS LOVE OF THE OUT-
DOORS TO HIS POTAWATOMI HER-
ITAGE, SCULPTOR DENNY HASKEW
LEARNED TO COOK ON RIVER TRIPS.
THE COLORADO-BORN ARTIST
STARTED RUNNING RIVERS IN HIGH SCHOOL AND ENDED UP WORK-
ING AS A BOATMAN AND COOK FOR AN EXPEDITION COMPANY.
Guiding people down the Grand Canyon and Cataract Canyon, or along the
Salmon River, Haskew had to be vigilant. But the real challenge came when
the boats pulled ashore. "We fed groups of up to twenty-four people three
meals a day. Short trips were easy. But those twelve-to eighteen-day trips
really tested us."

Not only did Haskew have to accommodate river-sized appetites, but he
also tried to vary his menu as much as possible. That's what made dishes
like "Down River Eggs" or "Up River Potatoes" so handy. Based on the sim-
plest of staples, they could be subtly transformed by wild asparagus, dill, or
watercress, picked on the spot.

Hefting his Indian and western-theme bronzes around the country, Haskew
can still eat river-style without worrying about calories. There are, however,

some sculptures he can't carry, like the twelve-to-fifteen-foot tall bronzes commissioned by the Kumeyaay tribe for their casino in Barona, California. These monumental works (including one figure modeled on his

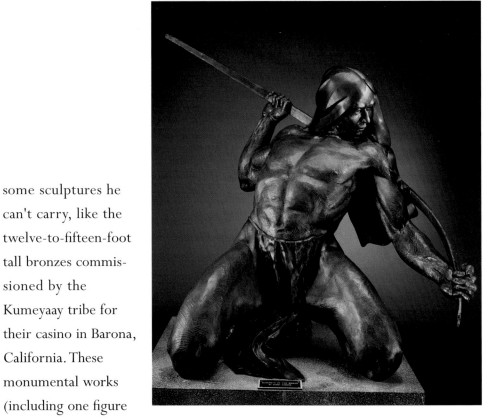

Strength of the Maker

Potawatomi grandmother) were hauled to Barona in semi-trailers and installed by crane.

A member of a thriving sculptors' colony in Loveland, Colorado, the artist recently built his own cabin overlooking a lake. He has taken up rowing again, and perhaps not suprisingly, one of his newer bronzes is a *"Food has always been wearable art to me."* boatman leaning affectionately on his oar. Is he thinking of cooking? Haskew laughs, "If you're a commercial boatman, you're always thinking of the people you have to feed."

UP RIVER POTATOES

6 potatoes (sliced)
1 large white sweet onion
milk or instant milk
Cheddar cheese

Place potatoes in a greased cast iron pot. Slice up one big sweet onion, and add it to the pot. Fill the pot almost to the top with watered-down milk or instant milk (you may use beer, but usually this will greatly offend beer drinkers).

Place the pot on a fire and allow the mixture to boil until it begins to douse the fire. Pull it off and drain. Fold in the sliced Cheddar cheese (which you should have sliced earlier), allow the cheese to melt, then serve.

DOWN RIVER EGGS

1 dozen eggs
6-8 green onions (diced)
8 oz. package cream cheese (cubed)
dash of garlic salt
dash of pepper

In a deep frying pan or cast iron pot, over medium heat, break a dozen eggs. Dice up green onions and cube a square of cream cheese, then add them to the eggs. Sprinkle with garlic salt and pepper to taste. With a flat spoon or spatula, stir the eggs, breaking the yolks. As the pot heats up, continue scraping the cooked eggs off the bottom and sides. As soon as the runniness appears to be gone, serve and eat.

CHARLIE PRATT

RAISED IN WESTERN
OAKLAHOMA BY HIS
CHEYENNE GRAND-
FATHER, SCULPTOR
CHARLIE PRATT, LIKE
MANY INDIAN KIDS, SUR-
VIVED ON SKILLET BREAD.
"I COULD ALWAYS CON
MY BROTHER, TONY, INTO
MAKING SOME WITH COM-
PLIMENTS ABOUT WHAT A
GOOD CHEF HE WAS." YET
PRATT HIMSELF ENDED UP COOKING A LOT OF THE TIME—ONE
REASON HE NO LONGER CARES TO COOK TODAY. "I DON'T LIKE
to cut grass or fool around in the garden, either. I had enough of that when I
was young," he emphasizes.

The artist, whose first hand-welded sculptures were done in an automotive
shop, now lives in Santa Fe, with movie stars and screenwriters for neighbors.
The native cultures of the Southwest inspire much of his work, along with

plant and animal subjects and his Plains Indian heritage. His combinations of brass and bronze with semi-precious stones make his work seem part sculpture and part jewelry.

Suprisingly, in the fiercely competitive Santa Fe market, no one has tried to imitate his work. The answer may lie in the fact that most of his pieces are based on painstaking patterns that can only be welded by hand. Indeed, though Pratt once built and oper-

"Food is like a box of chocolates—you never know what it might taste like."

ated a foundry for his work, he soon returned to a more intimate production method, using an acetylene torch to create his sculptures, leaving the seams rough and unfinished for effect.

And though he doesn't like to mow grass, he does like lawns—at least, the kind found on the golf course. "You know how people always say that when they retire, they're going to do nothing but play golf. Well, one time I tried to play golf for a week," he confesses. "I didn't make it. After about three days, I was exhausted—I couldn't move." For Pratt, playing golf full-time was harder than sculpting!

RED HOT BRATS IN BEER

6 fresh (uncooked) bratwurst
   (about 1 1/4 lb. total)
2 12 oz. cans beer
1 tablespoon hot pepper sauce
1 tablespoon Worcestershire sauce
6 frankfurter buns, split
2 teaspoons ground red pepper
2 teaspoons chili powder

optional: sauerkraut, pickles
   and mustard

Poke several holes in the skin of each bratwurst. In a large saucepan, combine bratwurst, beer, hot pepper sauce, Worcestershire sauce, red pepper and chili powder. Bring to a boil, then reduce heat. Simmer covered, about 20 minutes or until brats are no longer pink. Drain, cool. Chill for 4 - 24 hours.

At serving time: grill brats on an uncovered grill, turning frequently, directly over medium hot coals for 7 to 8 minutes, or until the bratwurst skins are golden. Serve on buns with sauerkraut, pickles or mustard, if desired. Or top with Pepper Pear Relish (see next recipe).

Makes 6 servings.

PEPPER PEAR RELISH

3/4 cup cider vinegar

1 small pear (peeled and finely
chopped)

1 red sweet pepper (finely
chopped)

1 onion (finely chopped)

4 oz. can diced green chiles
(drained)

1/4 cup sugar

2 teaspoons prepared mustard

1/8 teaspoon ground tumeric

In a saucepan, combine all the ingredients. Bring to a boil, reduce heat and simmer uncovered, for 30 minutes. Cool, cover and chill up to four days before using.

SKILLET BREAD

2 cups flour

1 teaspoon salt

1 tablespoon baking powder

1 cup warm water

Mix dry ingredients, make a well, add warm water, and mix until dough is just past the sticky stage. Pat out into three 8-inch patties about 1/2 inch thick. Add flour if the dough is still sticky. Cook in medium hot skillet until brown.

CHESSNEY SEVIER

BORN IN CASPER, WYOMING, WHERE
HER MOTHER ATTENDED COLLEGE
AND COMPETED IN RODEO AND HER
FATHER WAS A PROFESSIONAL BRONC
RIDER, CHESSNEY SEVIER HAD NO
DIFFICULTY DEVELOPING AN INTEREST
IN RODEO COMPETITION. OF
NORTHERN ARAPAHO DESCENT, SHE
GREW UP IN SENECA, NEBRASKA, RETURNING TO CASPER FOR
COLLEGE ON A RODEO SCHOLARSHIP. AT CHADRON STATE
College she mixed rodeo with art, completing her Bachelor's Degree in Fine Art.

Her specialty of intaglio printing has already begun to win acclaim at
juried shows. She has won awards for printmaking at Sioux Falls Tribal Arts,
and for two consecutive years at the Red Cloud Indian Art Show. Intaglio
printing was the one course Sevier took independent of her college studies,
but the method has become her favorite due to her enjoyment of the process
as well as the result.

Sevier does not consider herself a domestic type, and she has never developed
a passion for cooking, "but eating, on the other hand, is different." As a small child,

she favored the active life style, even in the kitchen. "I remember sticking my cold hands up the back of my grandmother's shirt while she was cooking, and she would yell, 'Oh, Annie!' and I would run and think I was so funny."

Living in a sparsely populated and isolated area, the artist considers herself very traditional. The Old World quality of intaglio printing is a perfect analogy for her creative thought process.

"Good wholesome food is the staff of life!"

FLAVOR CRAVOR DIP

1/2 cup Heinz Chili Sauce
1 8 oz. package Philadelphia
  Cream Cheese, softened
1/2 cup mayonnaise
1/4 cup chopped onion
1 can (4 1/2 oz.) tiny shrimp,
  rinsed and drained
creamed horseradish (optional)

Blend chili sauce gradually into cream cheese. Mix in mayo, add onion and a little horseradish if desired. Fold in shrimp. Cover and chill at least one hour.

Makes 2 1/2 cups. I always double this recipe.

I got this recipe from Evalyn Adamson. She fixes it for Christmas Day, New Year's, and during the Orange Bowl when Nebraska plays.

NELDA SCHRUPP

"AN ARTIST MUST BE A JACK-OF-ALL-TRADES—PHOTOGRAPHER, ADVERTISER, AND BUSINESS ACCOUNTANT," SAYS NELDA SCHRUPP. ADD TO THAT ART INSTRUCTOR AT TWO NORTH DAKOTA COLLEGES, AND YOU HAVE A CONCISE DESCRIPTION OF SCHRUPP HERSELF.

INSPIRED BY THE GEOMETRIC ART OF PLAINS INDIAN WOMEN AS WELL AS SUCH MODERN MASTERS AS BRANCUSI AND CALDER, SCHRUPP'S JEWELRY COMBINES HARD-edged shapes and soft, hollow ones. These become dramatic backdrops for semi-precious stones or natural, highly textured materials like horsehair and deer antler.

The results are what the artist describes as "amuletic forms"—small-scale sculpture and jewelry. Her silver and copper necklaces, for example, pay homage to the spiritual power of the rattle. Schrupp designs the sound of the necklaces by filling them with silver beads of varying sizes. But there is also an element of mystery involved: "Some necklaces refuse to take on a voice," she observes.

To support her jewelry making, Schrupp spends her days commuting

between Turtle Mountain Community College and United Tribes Technical College. Teaching a range of courses from Design to Art History, the artist often lunches in the school cafeteria. The food, she says wryly, is "full of calories—but warm." In Grand Forks, where winter temperatures drop to thirty below, "warm" counts for a lot.

On holidays, some of Schrupp's time is spent on meals that reflect her Metis (French/Indian) and Nakota (Sioux) ancestry. That means traditional New Year's dishes that unite "la boulette" meatballs and Indian frybread. Her husband, who travels to art shows with her, also takes over cooking when Schrupp is busy in her studio. Either that, or he'll knock on the door "to tell me it's time for supper. And then we'll go out to dinner," she laughs.

Amuletic Form with Audio Esthetics

"Food is sacred because it gives strength to the body and soul."

BOILED MEAT

1 1/2 lbs. chuck roast, cut into 1
to 2 inch cubes
6 medium potatoes, peeled and
quartered
half a large onion
salt and pepper

Boil meat, salt, pepper and onion until the meat is tender. Add potatoes, then boil until done. Serve the meat and potatoes on a plate with the meat juice. Mash the potatoes on your plate and mix the meat juice in like gravy.

Serve with fry bread and enjoy.

This is a very mild tasting meal.

DAVID TUNE

WHEN HE'S WORKING, ALBUQUERQUE JEWELER DAVID TUNE PREFERS FAST FOOD. "THE FASTER, THE BETTER, 'CAUSE I DON'T LIKE SITTING AROUND." ON SELLING TRIPS, HOWEVER, TUNE IS SO SELECTIVE ABOUT HIS MEALS THAT HIS DRIVING ROUTE IS PLANNED TO TAKE IN THE BEST RESTAURANTS ALONG THE WAY.

That "the best" need not be equated with "expensive" or "fancy" is something he learned from his mother, Hazel Houge Tune. Working at Taos Day School, Hazel could transform the most meager of staples into excellent Mexican food. His brother also learned to cook, but Tune himself is content to grill chicken or fish on occasion. Although he is of Hopi-Navajo descent, Tune's gift from his adoptive mother was the Creek heritage and language he has taken for his own.

This heritage is expressed in Tune's silverwork, incised with male/female Muscogee designs, incorporating opals as well as the more common lapis, coral and turquoise. During the jewelry-making process, he often reflects on numerous other lives entwined with his materials. "I smoke and pray for each

of them, especially the workers who mine the stones. I also pray that my stones bring happiness to the person they come to last."

This spiritual outlook has been partly nourished by his healer uncle, Marcellus Bearheart Williams, and reinforced by a near-fatal bout with cancer. "Before I had cancer, I did an art show every weekend for a year and a half. Cancer brought me back down to what's important." Putting ego and deadlines aside, Tune reached out to others, especially other artist friends. "When I was sick, I saw what art is really about," he says passionately. "Art is a form of healing."

"I love the ocean and a good In-and-Out Burger."

Green Chile Enchilada Casserole

1 can cream of mushroom soup

1 can cream of chicken soup

1/2 cup water as needed

4   8 oz. diced green chiles
     (frozen or canned)

1 dozen corn tortillas

1 small onion (diced)

2 1/2 cups Longhorn or mild
     Cheddar cheese (shredded)

2 cups cooked chicken (cubed)

Preheat oven to 350 degrees

Place the soups and green chiles in a saucepan (add water as needed). Stir ingredients together and bring the mixture to a boil. Turn heat off.

In a large casserole dish, place tortillas to cover the bottom. Sprinkle with cheese, add onions and chicken. Cover with the soup mixture. Repeat with another layer.

Bake the casserole for 30-60 minutes or until hot and bubbly.

My brother told me this is one my mother used to make. It was great.

FLAT ENCHILADAS

2-3 cups red chile sauce

6-8 corn tortillas

2-4 cups grated Longhorn or mild
    Cheddar cheese

1 medium red, white or yellow
    onion, diced

shredded lettuce for garnish

oven-proof plate for each person

Preheat oven to 350 degrees. Heat the chile sauce in a pan. To assemble each enchilada: place heated chile sauce on the plate and then place a tortilla in the sauce. Add onions and cheese to the tortilla, and then add more chile sauce. Repeat this until 3 to 4 layers have been made.

When the stacks are completed, pour the remaining sauce over the top and add more cheese and onions.

Bake for 10 minutes or until the cheese has melted.

Garnish with shredded lettuce.

For a variation, add browned ground beef, chicken or shredded pork to each layer.

Serves 2 people

This is my brother Tommy's recipe. I told him he should be a Chief, or is that Chef?

CONNIE TSOSIE GAUSSOIN

SOME ARTISTS WITH INTERTRIBAL BACK-
GROUNDS IDENTIFY MORE WITH ONE
NATION THAN ANOTHER. "I'M STRONG
IN BOTH MY TRIBES," SAYS JEWELER
CONNIE GAUSSOIN. "SEVERAL OF MY
AUNTS WERE RUG WEAVERS. I GET MY
TRADITIONAL NAVAJO DESIGNS FROM
THEM. BUT I USE A LOT OF PUEBLO DESIGNS, TOO."

USING THE TUFA CASTING TECHNIQUE WITH BOTH GOLD AND
silver, the Santa Fe jeweler prefers simple designs that emphasize texture.
Occasionally, her textures are so complex—from fine lines to deep cutout patterns—that the design itself is almost hidden in the texture.

Gaussoin herself stands out as a female jeweler in what has traditionally
been a male-dominated field. The bias she sometimes encounters is offset by
support from her husband and children, and her
work is constantly evolving in response to her sur-   *"Eat, drink, and buy art!"*
roundings. "I'm being influenced by the different
types of art shows we do, and the people who buy my jewelry. I've started

naming my major pieces because they make such a statement to me."

Nor is Gaussoin's background confined to arts and crafts. She spent her teen years performing with the "Up With People" show. Taking her high school classes by correspondence, she traveled from Canada to Panama to Scandinavia. She believes her travels exerted a major influence on her designs.

Unbeknownst to most, "Up With People" ran two cooking schools for program participants. "We learned to do all types of cooking—soufflés, marzipan and quiches," says the jeweler. Although she still cooks, her schedule no longer allows for a lot of complicated dishes. Confesses Gaussoin, "I even buy salads in bags 'cause you don't have to cut it up!"

CONNIE'S FAVORITE GREEN CHILE QUICHE

1 pastry pie shell (use your
   favorite recipe)

3 eggs

1 1/2 cups milk

1/2 teaspoon salt

pinch of pepper

1/2 to 1 cup grated cheddar cheese

1 small can diced green chiles
   (or roast your own)

Butter a lightweight piece of foil, press into pastry shell and fill with dried beans. Bake in 400 degree preheated oven for 8-9 minutes. Remove foil and beans. Prick the shell with a fork and return it to the oven for 2-3 minutes or until the shell begins to color. Reduce oven temperature to 375 degrees.

Quiche filling: Beat together eggs, milk, salt and pepper. Stir in green chiles and cheese. Pour mixture into partially cooked pastry shell, about 3/4 full to give the quiche room to puff. Return to the oven for approximately 30 minutes, or until an inserted knife comes out clean.

Serve hot. Makes 8 portions.

This recipe was given to Connie by a good friend in 1976. It was her favorite recipe and quickly became Connie's. Enjoy!

Variation: try tiny tart shells.

SALLY THIELEN

WHEN SALLY THIELEN'S FATHER BROUGHT HOME RACCOON, HER MOTHER COOKED THE MEAT AND SAVED THE GREASE TO FRY DONUTS. LESS INTERESTED IN COOKING THAN DECORATING, SALLY FROSTED THE DONUTS, THEN MADE DESIGNS IN THE FROSTING WITH HER FINGERS. "HUNTING AND TRAPPING PROVIDED FOOD AND MONEY FOR US," NOTES THE MIXED-BLOOD CHIPPEWA ARTIST. "IT REMINDS ME OF THE WAY OUR PEOPLE LIVED LONG AGO."

Specializing in three-dimensional works, the Michigan-based Thielen draws upon natural materials to create her ceramic masks and sculptures. Ever wonder what inspired her rabbit dolls?—"When I was four or five, I'd take the animals my dad has trapped before he skinned them out. I'd wrap them in blankets, put them in my doll carriage and pretend they were my pets."

Thielen's lively imagination was eventually channelled into her art, but she stayed away from cooking if there was nothing to decorate. When she did take time out from her artwork to prepare meals, "I'd walk away away from the stove and forget what I was cooking." That changed in 1996, when, exhibiting

her work in Japan, the artist was converted by the beauty and simplicity of Oriental cooking. "What I like best is that after the initial preparation, everything's cooked right before you, on the spot."

To counteract the effects of tasty meals, Thielen and her husband run regularly, even when traveling to shows. This is not a couple that gets tired setting up their booth; in fact, both plan to compete in the National Senior Olympics. Just how much stamina are we talking about?

"My father was a hunter and a trapper who provided food for us to survive. Most wild game and traditional foods inspire my work."

"Well," says Thielen, "We did a show in Arkansas one October and ran a twenty-six-mile marathon afterwards."

SUKI YAKI
(FROM SALLY'S FRIEND JUDY)

Buy a really good cut of beef, place it in the freezer until it starts to freeze. Remove it and slice very thin. Marinate the beef slices in brown sugar, a little soy and sake.

Thinly slice vegetables:

sweet potatoes

squash

eggplant

Use the following vegetables whole:

green onions

mushrooms (any variety)

Also include any of your favorites.

Place the meat in the center of a wok or large skillet, cook a little, adding more soy and sake. Add the sliced vegetables that take the longest to cook, and sprinkle the mixture with brown sugar.

Add semi-cooked Japanese noodles and the whole vegetables, keeping them in groups. Arrange the vegetables nicely for serving.

Serve each guest a raw egg in a small individual bowl. The guest should mix the egg with chopsticks, then from the central cooking pan take a small amount of the beef and vegetable mixture and dip it in the egg. Rice is also very good with this dish.

Quantities of meat and vegetables should be according to the number of guests.

Mom's Fried Muskrat

5 muskrat hindquarters and legs

Boil the meat in water for 30 minutes. Remove, coat in flour, and fry.

Add salt and pepper to taste. Cover with sliced onions and cook until the meat is done.

Serves a family of 4.

Mom's Raccoon Grease Donuts

2 eggs
1 cup sugar
1 cup sour milk
4 tablespoons melted shortening
1/2 teaspoon cinnamon
1 teaspoon baking soda
1 teaspoon nutmeg
pinch of salt
5 1/2 cups flour

Mix ingredients and roll out on a floured surface. Cut into donut shapes. Fry in hot raccoon grease (vegetable oil may be substituted) until golden brown. Frost or coat with powdered sugar.

Donut Frosting

Use a whole bag of powdered sugar, adding butter or grease. Flavor with one of the following: peanut butter, chocolate, vanilla, coconut. Also add a few drops of milk or water to improve the texture. Mix and spread carefully on donuts with a knife, then place them upside down in chopped nuts. Once in a while, I put sugar in a brown lunch sack and shake it to coat the donuts.

Raccoon grease donuts taste great and stay soft for at least a month when stored in a jar.

HAROLD LITTLEBIRD

WHEN HAROLD LITTLEBIRD FIRST STARTED MAKING FUNCTIONAL STONEWARE POTS, PEOPLE TOLD HIM HIS WORK WASN'T SANTO DOMINGO. HIS ANSWER? "WELL, I'M SANTO DOMINGO, AND I MADE IT." HE ALSO FIELDED CRITICISM THAT HIS POTS WEREN'T "TRADITIONAL" BY POINTING OUT THAT TRADITIONALLY, POTTERY WAS FUNCTIONAL. "I'M EXTENDING TRADITION," HE EMPHASIZES, "MAKING THINGS PEOPLE CAN USE."

Littlebird has always been an independent thinker, known for his poetry and music as well as his art. He grew up in a dual-career household; his father worked for the Southern Pacific Railroad in Oakland, California, and his mother for the Bureau of Indian Affairs in Brigham City, Utah!

At fifteen, Littlebird arranged to live in New Mexico with his brother, who worked at the Institute of American Indian Art. Littlebird attended school there, studying a number of design traditions, including those of his dual heritage, Santo Domingo and Laguna Pueblos.

While his geometric patterns, petroglyphs, and animal images may seem

Petroglyph Platter

familiar, a closer look reveals how unusual they are. Unlike the designs of most potters, Littlebird's only look painted. In fact, they're drawn with an underglaze pencil, a mineral oxide in pencil form. To make the designs permanent, Littlebird covers his pots with a simple, clear glaze he invented while he was a student.

A voice for maintaining an artist-friendly climate at Indian Market, Littlebird now mentors his wife and son-in-law as they explore their own pottery. Not only do they share studio space, they also take turns cooking. Busy frying rainbow trout from a recent fishing trip to Stone Lake, the potter says, "My work becomes more creative when the smell of food seeps into the studio!"

"All food is spiritual—share it with everyone!"

FISH MARINADE
(FOR GRILLED FISH)

This is a great summertime recipe for anyone who is interested in outdoor cooking, or for when you're camping. It works well with firm fish such as orange roughy or halibut, and I've used this marinade with salmon steaks and filets as well, with the same delicious results. Covers four or five filets.

1/4 to 1/2 cup light soy sauce or regular soy sauce thinned with water

1 to 3 garlic cloves, crushed

1/2 teaspoon basil leaves

2 to 3 pinches red chile powder

pinch of ground pepper

1 1/2 tablespoons Mongolian Fire Oil

2 to 3 tablespoons orange juice from canned concentrate

These are the main ingredients, but the amounts are approximate. Into a small baking dish or shallow pan, mix all the ingredients with enough light soy sauce to (pardon the pun) swim freely in the marinade. If you don't have light soy sauce, regular soy sauce will work if you thin it with a little water. The Mongolian Fire Oil is the trick to the marinade. It's made by the House of Tsaing. It has quite a bite, so suit to taste.

Turn the marinating fish every half hour or so, for two hours before grilling. Keep it covered and refrigerated between turnings. The remaining marinade may be brushed on while grilling. The fish is done when it flakes with a fork, but it takes about 7 to 10 minutes to a side when coals are white hot. Serve with a nice bottle of white wine and enjoy.

EDUARDO'S SALSA

This recipe was given to me by my late friend, Eduardo Lavadie, from Taos, New Mexico. Eduardo was a stickler for perfection, and after all his ingredients were chopped, diced or cut, then nothing metallic was ever allowed to touch the painstakingly prepared ingredients. I'm sorry, Eduardo, I was never such a purist, and I have to admit to you that I often use a hand-turned food chopper for my salsa, but I celebrate your memory each time I indulge in your delightful recipe.

6 to 7 firm Roma tomatoes, diced
1 to 2 regular tomatoes, squeezed
   to deseed, and then diced
1 finely chopped onion
3 to 4 cloves garlic, chopped
half a bunch fresh chopped
   cilantro (leaves only)

1 1/2 to 2 jalapeno peppers, finely
   chopped (more if your tummy
   can handle them)
pinch of salt (optional)
half a lime

About the jalapenos:
Eduardo used to say, "Pick out the soft, shriveled ones. For some reason they're the hottest." That tip, Eduardo, I religiously stick to, often going to two or three stores until I find the choicest ones.

EDUARDO'S WAY:

Mix all the prepared ingredients into a non-metallic serving bowl. Stir thoroughly with a wooden spoon or rubber spatula, finishing with the half a lime squeezed over the entire bowlful; then one final stirring. Serve with your favorite tortilla chips.

MY WAY:

With a food chopper or salsa maker. Same ingredients, less work.

Cut all the ingredients into halves or quarters. Place in a food chopper enough of each ingredient to fill it, then put on a lid and use a little mus-consistency. The more turns, the finer the mixture. Scoop the salsa into a non-metallic bowl and garnish with half a squeezed lime. Mix with rubber spatula and serve with your favorite tortilla chips.

Either way, add a few friends, a little reggae or Latino music, and you have all the right stuff for a festive party.

Red Chile Turkey Posole

This is a wonderful crock pot recipe. Nothing fancy, just a slow-cooked delight! It's great for potlucks, and especially tasty on cold, winter evenings. For those cutting back on fatty meats, turkey makes a delicious substitute for the more traditional pork version. It takes five to six hours on high heat, or overnight on low heat if you start in the evening. The posole absorbs a lot of water, so make sure you have a snug-fitting lid on your crock pot to prevent moisture from escaping. Even if some moisture escapes, adding a little water now and then does not hurt.

1 package of frozen posole (white corn leached with lime) Not canned hominy! or 1 pkg. of dry posole (has to be soaked 2 to 3 hours beforehand to soften)

1 1/2 to 2 lbs. diced turkey breasts or 1 1/2 to 2 lbs. ground turkey

1 to 2 onions, chopped

3 to 4 garlic cloves, chopped—more cloves if desired

1/2 teaspoon ground pepper

2 to 3 tablespoons ground red chile (heaping tablespoon, to taste)

1 bunch of freshly washed and chopped cilantro stems and leaves

1 teaspoon dried peppermint leaves (optional but tasty)

In a 6 quart slow cooker, add the thawed or soaked posole to 5 to 6 cups of water (crock pot on high). Add the chopped onions, garlic and pepper, cover, and continue to cook on high heat while in a separate frying pan you brown the turkey meat with a little canola oil. Drain and add the turkey meat to the posole. Cover and allow to cook for about another hour. Wonderful aromas will begin to waft through your kitchen. Add the chopped cilantro, red chile and peppermint leaves if desired, stir in, cover, and continue to cook on high for the remainder of the time. The posole will usually double in size or even burst open like popcorn when cooked this long. When serving, I will cut wedges of lime to squeeze into individual bowls. Salt to taste and complement with flour tortillas.

RICHARD AITSON

KIMBALL UNION ACADEMY, OBERLIN
COLLEGE, THE INSTITUTE OF AMERICAN
INDIAN ART—BEAD ARTIST RICHARD
AITSON'S FAR-FLUNG SCHOOLING—SUP-
PLIED THE MOTIVATION IN HIS LEARNING
TO COOK. IN COLLEGE, HE ORGANIZED A
THANKSGIVING DINNER FOR A INTERNA-
TIONAL GROUP OF STUDENTS, EXCEPT
THAT HIS TURKEY AND DRESSING WAS THE ONLY TRADITIONAL
FARE. LATER, HE TAUGHT HIMSELF TO COOK "BOTH OKLAHOMA
and Indian foods. That was my way to fight homesickness," he confides.

As with cooking, Aitson mastered his beadwork out of necessity, to finish
his gourd dance outfit when he was invited to join the Kiowa Gourd Clan. His
work is unusual in combining geometric and floral designs while conforming
to family guidelines learned from his grandmother and aunt.

He now specializes in beaded medallions, gourds, and miniature pieces such
as amulets. In1997, Aitson made history at the Red Earth Festival, becoming
the first artist to win a Grand Award for beadwork.

But Aitson keeps his focus not on personal achivement, but on the history
of his tribe and the Plains culture in general. He makes frequent visits to the

Palo Duro Canyon, in Texas, a hiding place for the Kiowa during the Plains Indian wars, and refuge for one of Aitson's ancestors, the famed warrior Goolayee. Home to three different kinds of cedar and sage, redolent with Indian perfume, the canyon is traversed by a stream that offers relief from steamy southwest summers. "It's a power-packed place," notes the beader. "All the plants the Kiowa used for food and medicine are in that canyon."

"As I get older, I feel more like a bottle of vintage wine; green and rusty around my neck and sediment in my bottom."

QUICK CHILI

Brown 2 lbs. ground chuck with one chopped large yellow onion. Drain the excess grease and add 1 teaspoon black pepper, 1 teaspoon salt, 1 teaspoon red chili pepper (New Mexico), 1/2 teaspoon ground cumin. Mix well and add a package of Hammett House Chili Mix, (an Oklahoma landmark restaurant located in my wife's hometown of Claremore). This can be found in most larger Oklahoma markets. Simmer for 15 minutes and add 2 8 oz. cans of tomato sauce and 1 can of Rotel chopped chiles and tomatoes. Add a little water if this is too thick. Cook for twenty minutes on medium low and serve on spaghetti, corn chips or in your biggest bowl topped with commodity cheese.

P.S. It tastes better the next day.

RICH'S FAMOUS KIDNEY ON A STICK

If you are grilling steaks, try this. Cut a kidney into sections and place with chunks of onion of the same size on wooden skewers (if you are a Plains Indian, save a section or two to munch raw while the meat cooks). Roast over coals until well done. Do not overcook, as the kidneys can become hard and dry if burned. A Kiowa favorite!!!

Rich Aitson's Ceremonial Brisket

Step 1:

Take the fat from a large brisket and marinate overnight in a mixture of Worcestershire sauce, freshly chopped onion, 1/2 teaspoon garlic and a can of beer.

Step 2:

Prepare 10 lbs. of charcoal until red and glowing. Add on top half a 5 lb. bag of hickory wood chips that have been soaking in water for 2 hours. The remainder will be added later.

Step 3:

With the coals & wood chips smoking, at precisely 12:00 midnight face east and sing four 49 songs. Place the brisket on a rack above a water basin over the wood chips. Add salt, pepper and sliced onion to the top of the brisket.

At precisely 4:00 AM, add the remaining wood chips. Add more water to the basin and turn the brisket over.

Return to bed.

At precisely 6:00 AM, once again face east and sing four more 49 songs, then remove the brisket from the smoker. Hide in a secure place, because your relatives will be hungry as they return from the 49 country. They will undoubtedly smell the remains of the brisket from over the fire, and if they find it, they won't leave any for dinner.

Serve with Selmon Brothers or Head Country Sauce.

BENJAMIN HARJO, JR.

BENJAMIN HARJO HAS ECLECTIC CULINARY TASTES, BUT THERE IS ONE PATICULAR CHEESE WHICH HE REFUSES TO ACKNOWLEDGE AS A FOOD. HE WAS ATTENDING AN EXPOSITION OF HIS WORK IN RENNES, FRANCE, AND HE AND OTHER NATIVE ARTISTS HAD STOPPED IN A BED-AND-BREAKFAST HOTEL. A TRAY CAME AROUND, COVERED WITH DESSERTS AND CHEESES, AND THE UNSUSPECTING HARJO TRIED A PIECE OF CHEESE. "IT WAS TERRIBLE—LIKE WEARING YOUR SOCKS and then putting them in your mouth!" he shudders.

The Seminole-Shawnee artist hasn't lost his taste for French food completely. But in the kitchen these days, he favors Southwestern cooking. That make sense for someone who spent part of grade school in Clovis, New Mexico and received his art training at Santa Fe's Institute of American Indian Art.

There he excelled in woodblock prints and gradually developed the painting style he is known for today. His witty puzzle designs--in traffic light colors—rely on the drafting triangle as well as the brush for their execution. So attention-grabbing are Harjo's designs, he was chosen by Absolut Vodka to paint his own version of their product for a national ad campaign.

"Market Morning and I Can't Find the Keys"

His inimitable style also finds expression in his attire—black beret, Mickey Mouse watch, funny socks. Not to mention Harjo's trademark laugh as he recalls his first failed cooking experiment on his grandparents' farm in Byng, Oklahoma. Both grandparents had gone shopping, so the ten year old decided to whip up a batch of sugar cookies. "There was just one problem. I used baking soda instead of sugar," he chuckles. "My grandfather nearly broke a tooth on one. He called them 'squirrel killer' cookies." That childhood spirt of fun, so essential for making art, has become so much a part of Harjo that it is reflected in his personality, his art and his cooking.

"Food should be consumed as rapidly as possible, just in case there are seconds."

Black Bean Burritos

1 lime

1 medium onion (chopped)

3 cloves garlic (chopped)

1/2 tablespoon olive oil

1 can black beans (do not drain)

1 can sweet corn (drained)

1 can diced peeled tomatoes
   (do not drain)

2 small chopped jalapenos
   (deveined and deseeded)

handful of fresh cilantro
   (chopped)

4 oz. each of Monterey Jack and
   Cheddar cheese (shredded)

8-10 large corn or flour tortillas

Sauté garlic and onion in olive oil until soft. Add beans, corn, tomatoes, jalapenos, lime juice and cilantro. Cook down 10-20 minutes. Roll the mixture into tortillas with shredded cheese and place in a casserole dish. Top with the remaining cheese, cover with foil, and cook until heated through at 350 degrees. Hmm, hmm, and good for you!

Serves 4-6

Green Chile Posole

2 cups posole

10 fresh roasted and chopped green chiles (deveined and deseeded)

2 medium chopped jalapenos (deveined and deseeded)

1 large onion (chopped)

3 cloves garlic (chopped)

2 teaspoons dried Mexican oregano

1 1/2 lb. pork loin (diced)

Rinse posole in cold water until the water runs clear. Soak for about 3-4 hours. Then place posole in a large pot, cover with water and bring to a boil. Reduce the heat and simmer on low until the posole begins to pop, approximately 1 hour, adding water as needed. Add chiles, jalapenos, onion, garlic, oregano and pork. Simmer covered for approximately 4 hours. Remove the meat and shred, then return it to the pot to continue cooking for at least an hour. This is a stand up and shout posole.

Serves 8-10

DRUNKEN SWEET ONION PIE

1 large deep dish pie shell

4 large sweet onions (Vidalias,
   1015s or Sugar Babies are best,
   when in season)

2-3 tablespoons butter

1 teaspoon olive oil

2 eggs

1/2 cup half and half

pinch of course ground pepper

2 oz. Swiss cheese (shredded)

generous pinch of nutmeg

handful of fresh parsley
   (chopped)

1/4 cup white wine

2 tablespoons brandy or cognac

Sauté onions in olive oil and butter until clear. Add parsley and pepper and continue cooking for 1-2 minutes. Add wine, brandy and nutmeg, cooking down the liquid. In a separate bowl, mix together eggs, half and half, and half of the cheese. Add the onion mixture and fold together. Place in the pie shell, cover the edges with foil, and top with remaining cheese. Bake at 375 degrees for 25-35 minutes.

Serves 6

VERONICA POBLANO

THE PEELED GREEN AND PURPLE PINK STONES OF VERONICA POBLANO'S JEW-ELRY RECALL A GARDEN OF PLANTS AND FLOWERS. EVEN THE NAMES OF THE STONES HAVE A VEGETAL RING— SUGILITE, ORVILLE JACK. BUT DON'T EXPECT TO RECOGNIZE ANY SHAPES. "I LIKE ABSTRACT OR SLIGHTLY ASYM-METRICAL DESIGNS," SAYS THE NEW MEXICAN JEWELER.

POBLANO'S FATHER, A ZUNI CARVER, WAS ALSO AN INNOVATOR— one of the first in his village to make animal and bird fetishes out of stone. Her mother did the inlay work. "I used to carve, too," says Poblano, "but the more I carved, the more I wanted to be a jeweler."

Even as a young girl, Polano admired the work of Hopi jeweler Charles Loloma and wanted to meet him; unfortunately, the meeting never took place. So she taught herself how to make jewelry, learning through her mistakes. "It took me a long time to master inlay without showing the fine lines between the stones."

Three of Poblano's children share her passion for jewelry making. Her

youngest, Dylan, also shares
his mother's enthusiasm for
creative cookery.

"I love to bake—pies, baklava,
homemade rolls," says Poblano.
"I cook mostly dishes with
pasta, vegetables, with olive oil
and garlic."

Some of the vegetables
come from the garden behind
her house in Zuni. "I have time
to garden because I don't watch
TV," she notes. In fact, despite
her unconventional designs, the
jeweler seeks balance in all
areas of her life, including her
art. She limits the number of
shows she does and the time
she spends on the road. "If you
do too many shows a year, your
work can get sloppy," she warns.

"Keep the refrigerator clean!"

CHOCOLATE VELVET CHEESECAKE

CRUST:

1 cup vanilla wafer crumbs

1/2 cup chopped pecans

3 tablespoons sugar

1/4 cup butter

Mix the ingredients together and press into the bottom of a 9 inch pan. Bake at 325 degrees for 10 minutes.

FILLING:

16 oz. cream cheese (softened)

1/2 cup packed brown sugar

2 eggs

6 oz. semi-sweet chocolate (melted)

3 tablespoons almond flavored liqueur

Beat together the cream cheese and brown sugar with a mixer at medium speed until well blended. Add eggs one at a time, mixing well after each addition. Blend in the chocolate and almond liqueur. Pour into the crust and bake at 475 degrees for 35 minutes.

TOPPING:

2 cups sour cream

2 tablespoons sugar

Mix sour cream and sugar until well blended. Carefully spread on cheesecake, then bake ten minutes more.

Loosen cheesecake from the rim of the pan while still warm. Cool before removing. Refrigerate and garnish with chocolate leaves or shaved chocolate.

VERONICA'S SAUTÉED GREEN BEANS WITH ROASTED PIÑON NUTS

2 pounds fresh green beans

1/4 cup olive oil

1 cup piñon nuts (shelled)

garlic salt to taste

Parmesan cheese (optional)

In a large skillet, toast the piñon nuts on low heat, tossing continuously, to a light toast. Set aside in a small dish. In the same skillet, pour olive oil over the green beans and toss to coat the beans well. Add the piñon nuts and toss again. Add a dash or two of garlic salt and place in a baking dish. Bake at 350 degrees for 20 to30 minutes. Add a sprinkle of Parmesan if you like for the last three minutes of baking.

INDEX OF RECIPES

BREADS

DRESSINGS, MARINADES, RELISHES AND SAUCES

DESSERTS

INDEX OF ARTISTS